❧ LETTER FROM MOROCCO

Letter from Morocco

Christine Daure-Serfaty

❧ *Preface by* EDWY PLENEL

Translated by
PAUL RAYMOND CÔTÉ &
CONSTANTINA MITCHELL

Michigan State University Press
East Lansing

Copyright © 2003 by Michigan State University Press

♾The paper used in this publication meets the minimum requirements of ANSI/NISO Z39.48–1992 (R 1997) (Permanence of Paper).

Michigan State University Press
East Lansing, Michigan 48823–5245

Printed and bound in the United States of America.

Originally published as *Lettre du Maroc*, ©Éditions Stock, 2000.

Published with the cooperation of the French Ministry of Culture—National Center of the Book.

09 08 07 06 05 04 03 1 2 3 4 5 6 7 8 9 10

LIBRARY OF CONGRESS CATALOGING-IN-PUBLICATION DATA
Daure-Serfaty, Christine.
[Lettre du Maroc. English]
Letter from Morocco / Christine Daure-Serfaty; preface by Edwy Plenel; translated by Paul Raymond Côté and Constantina Mitchell.
    p. cm.
ISBN 0-87013-687-9 (pbk.)
1. Serfaty, Abraham. 2. Daure-Serfaty, Christine. 3. Political prisoners—Morocco—Biography. 4. Morocco—Politics and government—1961–1999. I. Title.
DT325.92.S47D3813 2003
964.05'2'092—DC21
                                                  2003009752

Book design by Valerie Brewster, Scribe Typography
Cover design by Heather Truelove Aiston

Visit Michigan State University Press on the World Wide Web at:
www.msupress.msu.edu

To my friends

ℰ CONTENTS

❦ *Preface*

I once read that there was no such thing as instant friendship.

That was in 1993. The statement had been made by the writer Maurice Blanchot, a very private man by nature. From the realm of his infinite secrecy, he had set out to refute Montaigne, whose explanation of his sudden fondness for La Boétie ("Because it was he, because it was I") was, Blanchot confessed, "more annoying than touching." "There's no such thing as instant friendship. Bonds are formed little by little as a result of the slow workings of time," Blanchot retorted. "We were friends but didn't know it."

Clearly, Blanchot was expressing that view in homage to a friend, Dionys Mascolo, one-time companion of Marguerite Duras. It appeared in Blanchot's preface to the final collection of Mascolo's essays, *À la recherche d'un communisme de pensée* (In Search of a Communism of Thought). By virtue of its discretion and restraint, Blanchot's tribute is far more loyal and true than many an emotional outpouring. His text (or "pre-text," as he calls it) makes us privy to an unspoken camaraderie intertwining politics and writing, full of commitments and refusals, silent anger and open resistance, particularly during the Occupation and the Algerian War. The title Blanchot gave his preface to Mascolo's last book was simple and unassuming: "In the Name of Friendship."

One preface leads to another. I too am writing in the name of friendship—not out of friendship, but on the concept of friendship. Nevertheless, I'd like to refute Blanchot's statement, because I did in fact see instant friendship in Nicole's eyes early one morning in 1976 or '77. I don't remember the exact date anymore, or the circumstances, or even what was said. But I distinctly remember the look in her eyes—like a bright flash of light—and the unusual sound of her voice. Her words conveyed not only her enthusiasm, but also her surprise at being enthused so quickly, casting aside caution and hesitation. Nicole had just come home in the wee hours of the morning, after spending a good part of the night talking with a stranger. Suddenly freed of the guise of formality that normally shielded her, she was literally overwhelmed by friendship.

Nicole Lapierre, the woman I love, had just met Christine Daure, who had not yet become Christine Daure-Serfaty. It was through Christine and her radiance that Nicole also came to know Abraham, held captive for three years in the shadows of a faraway prison cell. He was to spend another fourteen years there, condemned by a monarch who ruled by divine right.

꙳

I've really only been a witness to all this—a witness to the plotting of women. A remarkable conspiracy. One of those conspiracies that governments, kings, princes, and ministers can do nothing to stop: a conspiracy grounded in friendship.

The earliest tangible evidence of this amateur conspiracy hatched among friends was the first issue of a little-known periodical, the short-lived feminist journal *La Revue d'en face* (*The Review from the Other Side*), which appeared in May 1977. It had been nearly ten years since the May '68 protests in France, and disenchantment was in the air. Defining itself as "a feminist political review," the journal sought to create nothing less than a "different brand" of politics. It was a mammoth undertaking: one that all the other "different politics" of various parties — past and future — would never fully achieve. The journal's inaugural issue was graced with a cover drawing by the Moroccan artist, Chaïbia. In the section entitled *Terre des femmes* (*Women's Land*)[1] was an article on "women's liberation in the desert," which focused on the struggle of the Saharawi women. It was co-authored by Nicole and a mysterious "C. J." — who in reality was Christine. At the time, she was going by "Jouvin," her second husband's name.

"C. J.": those two initials were the first written indication of the beginning of a friendship that was to make us better people than perhaps we really are. What I mean is that the relationship was not motivated solely by friendship, but by compassion as well.

The instant friendship Nicole experienced happened during an interview she had arranged with Christine to get information to supplement what she had learned on a trip to the Saharawi camps. Or it might have been in preparation for the trip; I can't remember which. In August of 1976, following

1. Translators' note: The phrase is a play on the title of Antoine de Saint-Exupéry's 1939 novel, *Terre des hommes*.

three months of house arrest and at least fifty interrogation sessions, Christine had been deported from Morocco for having hidden Abraham. The chief crime of his organization had been defending the former Spanish Sahara's right to self-determination. During the course of the interview, Nicole and Christine exchanged opinions about the desert, women, politics, men . . . And the conversation is still going on.

Witnessing their collusion, I couldn't help but become their accomplice.

This personal story about a universal cause touches on liberty, liberties, and liberations. In other words, it deals with principles, rights, and individuals. While I merely played the role of smuggler, it was the tireless resistance of women, in the face of the overwhelming male power embodied by the reign of His Royal Majesty Hassan II, that can doubtless never be praised enough. The resistance of one woman in particular: Christine Daure-Serfaty. I have the joy and honor of writing the preface to *Letter from Morocco* today precisely because the secret weapon of her resistance was the written word.

But there's no cause for secrecy anymore: the end result of our friendly plotting was a book. A book denouncing a king. A book crafted like a time bomb. A book that would cause much more than an uproar: a book that would silence the absolute monarch. An irreverent and benevolent book. A book that by its very transgressions would be a demonstration of love for Morocco and its people.

The book was *Notre ami le roi* (*Our Friend the King*), published in 1990, and it was Nicole and Christine who came up with the idea of writing it.

❦

At the time, I was managing a series at Éditions Gallimard, and I wanted to publish a book detailing how France had failed the Moroccan people. No one was better equipped to write it than Christine. Her struggle on behalf of missing persons and prisoners, the living dead in the cells of Tazmamart and the torture victims of Kenitra, had led her countless times through the labyrinth of deal-making and corruption. She made inquiries and gathered information, searched for weak spots, broke down barriers, slipped through bureaucratic cracks and crevasses no matter how minute, pressured authorities, and impressed everyone with her candid manner and radiant eyes. Her soft voice masked an unwavering determination as fresh and pure as an adolescent's.

But Christine couldn't reveal her involvement without jeopardizing everything. In 1986, after being barred from the country for ten years, she was finally granted permission to return to Morocco. She married Abraham in prison and subsequently visited him and his fellow inmates on a regular basis. It was the beginning of a precarious situation, since Christine had obviously made no promises or guarantees in exchange for such a basic right, and she was well aware that her freedom to exercise that right depended on Hassan II's good will. She would need to be clever, keep up appearances, take extra precautions, continue her activism even more secretively and stealthily than before. Consequently, Christine's first book, *Rencontres avec le Maroc* (Encounters with Morocco), was published under the pseudonym "Claude Ariam."

Our friendship-based conspiracy needed more players. We had to broaden our bases. Find someone with a name to be our partner—another conspirator. We made the right choice. Gilles Perrault alone was worth an entire army in so many ways—and that's an understatement. In the offensive that was to follow, Gilles ended up playing all the parts: general and private, staff and infantry, aviation and artillery. Without him—without his talent as a writer, his devotion as an activist, and tenacity as a fighter—an amateur operation such as ours could never have shaken Hassan II's reign to the extent that it did.

After a day of brainstorming, Nicole was the one who suggested asking Gilles. He had authored *The Red Orchestra*, a monumental work commemorating a globalized Resistance that transcended countries and borders. Christine corroborated Gilles' continued support for the cause of the Moroccan people. He always backed petitions and campaigns, and maintained discreet but regular correspondence with one of Abraham's friends, held prisoner in Kenitra. I was entrusted with the mission of contacting him, armed with nothing but a single argument of my own invention—the title of the book we wanted to write: *Our Friend the King*. In the span of a train ride from Caen to Paris, my argument miraculously brought down the illustrious author's last barriers of defense.

The rest of the story belongs to Gilles and Christine.

Gilles is a slave to writing, a monolith of self-discipline, and a mountain of experience. He was totally in his element. Christine supplied him with notes, information, documentation, evidence, testimonials: the raw materials he ultimately molded, sculpted, and set into motion—infusing them with his own unique music, clarity, and rhythm. That was the secret recipe for *Our Friend the King:* the secret that bound our friendship, the secret that Gilles divulged so subtly in 1992, when the paperback edition came out. The book had achieved its purpose, and Gilles could now give Christine credit: he stated on the flyleaf that the book was the product of a "team effort" with her.

Looking back on the escapade, I remember it to have been much like a commando operation. Tasks were strictly assigned, supplies shared fairly, and we all pledged to bring the fight to its conclusion. The military metaphor is intentional. Thrilled to be on a mission where there was no turning back, that had no rear guard or reinforcements, Gilles Perrault instilled in us his deep determination, which was as fierce as it was generous. He seemed to have found an opportunity to reconcile his passion for writing with his taste for adventure, to appease the inner conflict of the man and the writer, while at the same time putting them both in jeopardy—since they were, after all, one and the same.

Writing is always a dizzying experience. You never know where it will lead. But even before the manuscript was finished, *Notre ami le roi* brought forth an additional challenge. Overriding our caution and brushing aside our reservations, Gilles never stopped reiterating to us that the goal of this one little book was—pardon the oversimplification—to defeat the monarchy, to cause its symbolic collapse under the weight of its crimes and their disclosure. He promised that, as a result of what he would write, fear would take the other side, and it would be the Makhzen's turn to be gripped with fright in the face of the army of specters he was going to raise, resuscitating through his words the ghosts of all those who had been victimized, assassinated, poisoned, imprisoned, tortured, and those who had disappeared: the dead and the living dead who would soon demand justice.

And he kept his promise. We know that now.

Notre ami le roi was available in bookstores by mid-September 1990. In February 1991, the Oufkir family was released. (To punish the betrayal of one man, his wife and children had been deprived of their freedom by order of the king.) In May and August, hundreds of Saharawis, who had been held in solitary confinement without a trial, were liberated. Nine young prisoners, including hunger strikers, were also returned to their families in August. On September 13th, Abraham Serfaty was removed from the prison in Kenitra and put on a plane bound for France. On the night of September 15, 1991, the twenty-eight surviving detainees in Tazmamart prison were pulled from the dungeons that served as their cells. The following morning, they were overwhelmed by the light of day. They hadn't seen it in eighteen years. In December of that same year, the three Bourequat brothers were allowed to return to France. They too had disappeared eighteen years earlier, without so much as a trial.

A single book has probably never before accomplished so much good. By that, I mean concrete good, on a tangible human level, in terms of lives saved.

With all due respect to cynics and skeptics, great intellectuals, and those accustomed to such events, my first inclination is simply to say: It was a good deed.

There were moments of tension and exasperation. That was unavoidable. After all, who were we in the face of the army of sycophants and opportunists, conspirators and palm-greasers, wheeler-dealers and profiteers, networks and offices that had always monopolized Franco-Moroccan relations? Yet my only recollection now is the rare sensation—the childlike joy—of a cause without bitterness, a camaraderie unmarred by quarreling.

Yes, that's what it was. A childlike joy.

ℰ

Childhood. Remaining true to childhood.

Abraham and Christine confronted their own childhood memories and joined their voices together in the superb book they co-authored, *La Mémoire de l'autre* (Memory of the Other), published in 1993. Her childhood was darkened by anxiety, and his was brightened by happiness, but the result was the same: two dissimilar childhoods, which have nevertheless merged to constitute the driving force of their mutual and uncommon strength.

Abraham says it was while watching his life pass before him, beneath the blindfold he was forced to constantly wear during the months following his arrest and incarceration in Casablanca's Derb Moulay Cherif prison, that he came to realize to what extent his childhood and adolescence "had been infused with happiness." Concerning the 1940s, he even goes so far as to write: "While a terrible darkness descended over Europe, and war was ravaging the world, I was paradoxically surrounded by light." He speaks of "privilege" and "fairy godmothers"; confides that he and his sister were "showered with affection" by their parents; describes his loving father returning from the market and exclaiming to the family in Hakitia, the Hispanic dialect of Jews in Northern Morocco: "Todo lo bueno!" And indeed, Abraham had "the best of everything." I would venture to say that it was by drawing from that emotional well that he was able to face the worst. There is no formula for withstanding torture, he wrote—in one of the few texts where he looks back on the nightmare that will forever hold a part of him prisoner: "What vomit is now buried within my flesh and guts?" But he adds, speaking from experience, that some precautions can be taken: "First and foremost, do not fear death; never fear death again."

Do not fear death. Abraham expresses that conviction without a hint of boastfulness, as simply and firmly as he has lived it—with the calm certitude of a child conscious of having been loved, of having experienced happiness.

The childhood Christine describes is the exact opposite: neither serene nor idyllic. But rather than dismiss it, she embraces it: "I don't have very many recollections, and the ones I do have are a burden, but I wouldn't trade them for anything. They make up my being from head to toe." Regardless of what she may say about the wounds and heartbreak, silences and deprivation, she realizes that despite the shellfire and fear, despite the fact that the house was bombed, and day became indistinguishable from night, she will always be true to the memory of her adolescence. It's a memory she shares as if in passing, as if it were a matter of course, because it was, in fact, a matter of course. "Naturally, my father was in the Resistance." He wasn't just any Resistance fighter. Pierre Daure was one of the few high-ranking government officials in education who spoke out against the regulations governing the status of Jews. As a result, he was dismissed from his duties by the Vichy government. After the Liberation, he became the first administrative head of the Calvados jurisdiction. He got involved in the Resistance instinctively, and at a time when the truth was not yet evident to the majority of the French population. It was the same natural instinct that prompted Christine to say "yes," "yes" with no questions asked, when it was suggested that she hide a member of the Algerian National Liberation Front in France toward the end of the 1950s. And again, that natural instinct made her say "yes" in Casablanca in the early 1970s when she was asked to hide Abraham, although she didn't even know him. She didn't hesitate for a moment, because to refuse, she says, "would have been like agreeing to have my father arrested."

"What good is it to bring children into this world if we don't somehow try to make it a better place for them?" she asks in the course of her dialogue with Abraham, written with intensity, discretion, care, and forethought. "That's what our parents did for us, and it was the best thing they did for us. The rest of it—family life, traditions—wasn't all that great, really."

Two childhoods, two worlds—and yet, the same lucidity, the same strength, the same heroism.

Christine and Abraham, our heroes.

Ordinary heroes.

Simple heroes.

Natural heroes.

Christine was instinctively able to say "yes" when she was asked to hide Abraham, and Abraham was ready to say "yes" to death when he had to face torture because both of them knew how to say "no." No to injustice. No to terror. No to oppression. And consequently, by logical extension, no to Morocco's king.

Those who said no . . . A certain segment of France's population today only speaks of its heroes in the past tense. It bemoans the country's bygone glory and illustrious dead, and broods over its former acts of courage to justify complaining about imaginary sacrifices. It ruminates over obscure and distant defeats instead of becoming involved in current problems. And yet, among that segment's eminent representatives, many were quick to say yes to the monarch, and therefore to the injustices, terror, and oppression he fostered while Abraham and Christine were saying no. Simply no.

I cannot emphasize enough how heroic it was to say no.

That's what Abraham and Christine have taught us: to be able to say no, without self-interest or calculation. They've taught us to refuse to make do, settle for less, or become apathetic—even when everything compels us to do the contrary. Even when we are given all the excuses we need; even when everyone tries to prevent us. After all, when Abraham endured the hell of Derb Moulay Cherif prison, he was already forty-eight. He had a family—a sister and a son (who were later arrested as well). And Christine, at the time, had a career, a second husband, and three children. She was leading a comfortable life, working for a government agency assisting developing countries. They both had every reason imaginable —ordinary, everyday reasons—to back out or give in. But they chose to believe there were other reasons, just as simple and just as ordinary, for doing the opposite.

And that's how they became heroes.

ᧉ

"I'm not afraid of what people are usually afraid of. The only thing I fear is fear."

On the last page of *À La recherche d'un communisme de pensée,* Dionys Mascolo quotes Hölderin, echoing the opening statement of Maurice Blanchot's preface on friendship. Referring to the intense excitement kindled by their commitments, Mascolo reminds Blanchot of the description the latter gave of their relationship: "We were brought together by the most unfailing, the most relentless of bonds: the friendship that comes of saying no."

The friendship that comes of saying no . . . Despite the similar chord Blanchot's definition strikes with what I've been talking about, I'm not sure it applies to our particular conspiracy, grounded in friendship. And it's even less suited to describe what Abraham Serfaty has represented for us in terms of image and stature over the past twenty years. Blanchot's premise suggests closure, a shutting in, a withdrawal from the world and others. Abraham is the total opposite. He is all openness and inquisitiveness, generosity and humanity. These words may seem outdated to the point of being obsolete, but I've used them intentionally, because they don't waver. It is precisely because they stay the course, impervious to showoffs and big talkers, that they so befit Abraham.

He could have an infinite number of legitimate reasons to be consumed with loathing and hate, to hold a grudge against the world and humanity, wall himself up in bitterness, live in the past and refuse to look to the future. But that kind of behavior is completely foreign to him. He was a communist when the Berlin wall came down; yet he viewed the event not as a defeat, but as a liberation—the removal of a sinister obstacle from the path of the eternal hope of those who had been subjugated, the turning of a new page that impostors and deserters had not already blackened. He defines himself as an Arab Jew, yet has eschewed the apparent security of Zionism, preferring to fight anti-Semitism on Muslim soil. Considered a traitor or enemy by extremists on both sides, he nonetheless refuses to play the role of prophet of doom and would rather go along with the Oslo Accords, despite their imperfections. The simple fact that Abraham favors a republic makes him a revolutionary in a country where the king's enormous powers are bolstered by an indomitable triad: the Caliph, Sharif, and Makhzen. Yet he agreed to take a chance on the social and democratic process put in motion by the death of Hassan II and by Mohammed VI's immediate disassociation, by way of statements and deeds, from his father's reign, even though the new king continues to rule by divine right.

There isn't an ounce of animosity, resentment, or hatred in Abraham.

In *Letter from Morocco*, Christine tells of Abraham's return to his homeland and, in doing so, reminds us of the legacy of Antigone: being able to say no to authority, the king, the government. Indeed Antigone—Sophocles' Antigone—states: "I am not of those who hate. I was born to love." And what if, all things considered, heroism were on the side of love, that inner peace that does not automatically predicate violence and war?

Love instead of hate. Life instead of death. Love that helps make it possible to risk one's life, to resist, and to fight. Life worth defending to the death.

"Your eyes are the sky, your mouth honey, your soul the sun." From his prison cell, Abraham wrote those words one day for Christine. Later, he added that, confined within those four walls, he had the impression that his precarious existence and uncertain future were completely enveloped by Christine's soul, "that enchanted soul that I'd yearned for since my earliest youth, that I'd been dreaming of since my first prison sentence forty-two years ago, that I'd imagined through Romain Rolland's character—Anne, and that has become a reality, thanks to you, Christine."

Love, like friendship, can happen in an instant.

Women are more aware of that than we men are. They let us profess our love, but they would rather experience it.

By recounting Abraham's return as she experienced it, Christine is professing her love in this book.

Reading it gives one a sense of the alchemy of their relationship. It's easy to deduce that Abraham's optimism could lead him into trouble, were it not for Christine's vigilance; that the enthusiasm of one is counterbalanced by the clear-headedness of the other; that between eagerness and apprehension, caution and audacity, they have above all learned to listen to each other.

I would like to stress that last point because I don't believe it to be self-evident. Even less self-evident is the fact that this joining of two free spirits—a woman defiant of male authority and a man defiant of a king's authority—could stand the test of hardship and blossom in an atmosphere of mutual respect.

There can be no doubt that our two heroes have broken with tradition: they've learned how to stay in love.

ॐ

When Christine writes about Morocco, the words that flow from her pen invariably evoke light.

Sun. Brightness. Whiteness. Shimmering. Light is constantly present, even in its opposite: the shadow of yesterday's terrors, the darkness of today's concerns.

One day soon, we will journey toward Morocco's light. Until now, we had deprived ourselves of it. There could be no Morocco so long as Abraham was not allowed to live in his homeland and pay homage at his parents' grave. But in retrospect, our attitude was a self-centered one, because that light was already shining on us.

A rare light. An earthly light. The light radiating from Christine and Abraham.

Edwy Plenel
Paris, March 26, 2000

❦ LETTER FROM MOROCCO

❦ Summer of '99

This is a story: very simply, the story of what I've experienced since the summer of 1999, and am still experiencing to this day. Is it a personal story? Of course it is, because I'm part of it. I've watched. I've listened. And now, it's time for me to write. But it's really Abraham's story I want to tell. And the story of Morocco—a country that has changed and continues to change daily before my eyes.

First, a few words about Abraham's childhood. The press hasn't given it much attention, yet it's the foundation on which he built his character. He was born in Casablanca in January, 1926—the second child of a Jewish Moroccan family whose firstborn was a daughter, Evelyne. His parents were first cousins on the Serfaty side, originally from Tangier. His father was a wholesale household appliance distributor. He was tall and strong, with a resounding voice, and was known for his hot temper and generous heart, as well as for his nationalist and progressive views. He was quite a character. Abraham's mother was a petite woman who had a strong personality as well. She doted on her family, but also gave of her time to others, working for charitable organizations two days a week. Reaching out to others the way Abraham and Evelyne's parents did was rare in Jewish Moroccan families, and the two children inherited the trait, subsequently incorporating it into their own way of life.

Evelyne was short and slight like her mother. She adored her brother. Abraham can still remember one of the first apartments they lived in downtown, above a pastry shop where he used to buy candy. He also remembers the beach nearby, where their mother would take them to play. The beach and ocean waves were among his earliest pleasures. Then the family moved into a house by a vacant lot that quickly became a playground for all the neighborhood children. There was a spot for repairing bicycles in the yard, and they spent a lot of time there, too. In the evening, Abraham and his sister did their homework in their rooms, which were within earshot of their mother, who was usually busy in the kitchen. Abraham's memories are studded with candied fruits and cakes. And how could he forget the bicycle that made it possible for him to zoom off to the beach? Their parents didn't play favorites as far as he and Evelyne were concerned. They loved and pampered both their children equally, worrying that Abraham was growing too quickly and that Evelyne was too tiny.

Even though Evelyne was quick and bright, it wasn't long before she was barred from school because of "quota limitations": the Vichy government had imposed the same anti-Semitic laws in Morocco as it had in France. Consequently, she helped her parents and followed in her brother's footsteps each time he took up a cause. Abraham was tall like his father.

He was a brilliant student, so he wasn't affected by the quota limitations. He passed his exams and was accepted into the National School of Mine Engineering in Paris. He still remembers his first boat trip to France, just after the war, and how surprised he was at the lingering severity of daily life there.

It is from that childhood—a Moroccan childhood—that Abraham was exiled.

ᘐ

When he was eighteen, well before he left for Paris, Abraham joined the Moroccan communist youth organization. After finishing his studies in France, he returned home, where his involvement in the Moroccan communist party and the fight for independence took precedence over his career goals. As always, Evelyne was there at his side. In 1953, they were both deported from Morocco by the French Protectorate. Nationalist militants were considered to be undesirables. In order to justify Abraham's deportation, the authorities claimed he was a Brazilian national (Abraham's father had worked in Brazil at a very early age and therefore had Brazilian papers). Moroccan officials used the same excuse to deport Abraham again in 1991. At the time of his first expulsion, Abraham was a young man. He was married and the father of a baby boy. The exile lasted three years. In the interim, Morocco became independent. When he and Evelyne returned, the minister of justice, Abdelkrim Benjelloun-Touimi, certified their Moroccan nationality. Abraham joined Morocco's first government, headed by socialist leader Abderrahim Bouabid, during the reign of King Mohammed v. After that, he was named technical manager at the state-owned phosphate mining office (the OCP: Office Chérifien des Phosphates). He loved working there and still talks about it today.

Then, oppression and political instability took hold of Morocco, and Abraham began his descent into darkness. Within the span of a few short years, he lost a prime career position and became a fugitive in his own country. Although he was Jewish, he took the side of the Palestinians during the Six-Day War in 1967, a decision that cut him off from his community. In 1968, he sent a letter to all the engineers at the OCP to voice his support of the miners on strike. He was removed from his post at the helm of the OCP and downgraded to the mining division. In 1970, he quit the Moroccan communist party and took all its student members along with him. They formed another organization, Ila Al Amam (meaning "onward"), which was never legally recognized. In 1972, he escaped the first wave of arrests, but refused to go into exile, choosing instead to go into hiding. That lasted until November, 1974. I think it's probably general knowledge that once Abraham was arrested, he and his comrades spent fifteen months in isolation at the Derb Moulay Cherif detention center, where they were tortured under the most atrocious conditions. He was subsequently sentenced to life imprisonment, transferred to the long-term prison in Kenitra, and "pardoned" seventeen years later, in 1991 — only to be again banished from the country, once more presumably because he was "Brazilian" . . .

While he was in hiding, his sister Evelyne sent him money. After several months, she was arrested by the police and brutally tortured. They tried to force her to tell them what she knew. She could have revealed names, but she never did. She died two years later, shortly after contracting a virulent form of hepatitis, without ever seeing her beloved brother again. She is buried in the Jewish cemetery in Casablanca, as are her parents. I've always felt she's been more or less forgotten: that her memory hasn't been honored as it should be. Evelyn and her father died while Abraham was in hiding; his mother, while he was in prison. He couldn't attend any of their burials—couldn't be there to mourn them.

It is also from these things—a cherished family (a Moroccan family), deaths unmourned, abandoned graves (Moroccan graves)—that he was exiled.

ᛦ

On September 30, 1999, Abraham finally returned to his homeland. After so much injustice, persecution, and suffering, I couldn't believe how Morocco opened its arms to him. People flocked from all over. He was on television and in the newspapers. People recognized him walking in the street, or passing by in a car. They greeted him, invited him to their homes and public gatherings. He was applauded and celebrated. Everyone wanted to have a picture taken with him. His return was the first clear sign of the change they'd been so anxiously awaiting. And he wanted to take in every aspect of his country—couldn't get enough of it. It had been twenty-six years since he'd lived as a free citizen here: over a third of his life. All he'd seen of his native land during the seventeen years he'd spent shut away in Kenitra was a patch of sky framed by prison walls—always the same sky, cut by the flight of birds and passing clouds. Only the light changed as the day progressed. And sometimes, he'd catch a glimpse of things through the mesh openings of the van that occasionally transported inmates to the hospital in Rabat. For nearly six years, every time we were together in the prison's visiting room, I could see a palm tree through the bars of the window, swaying in the breeze above the rooftop, just like in the poem.[2] It's true; I swear. Perhaps all prisons are like that. With the exception of what printed matter he could get his hands on, the only news Abraham had about his country came from what he heard in the visiting room. Topics of conversation were inevitably subjective, and carefully chosen so as not to discourage the Kenitra prisoners.

Later, during his eight years of forced exile in France, and over the course of his travels in Europe made possible by his political refugee status (we are truly grateful to France for having granted it), it was from afar that news of his homeland reached him. The anguish of his exile gave him a clear view of the situation and hardened his position.

And then, all of a sudden, that summer of '99, Morocco's doors opened to him, and he returned home. I came with him to begin the third phase of my Moroccan experience.

During the first phase, from 1962 to 1976, I had my children with me—all three of them. As I became familiar with Tangier, I was overwhelmed by the city and by the beauty of

2. Translators' note: The author is referring to the opening lines of a poem written by the nineteenth-century French poet, Paul Verlaine, while he was in prison: "Le ciel est, par-dessus le toit, / Si bleu, si calme! / Un arbre, par-dessus le toit, / Berce sa palme." (The sky over the roof is so blue, so calm. A tree, over the roof, lulls its branches.)

so many things there: the almost deserted beaches of sand and rock to the east, around Cape Malabata, and to the west at the foot of Cape Spartel and the Caves of Hercules. They were still cutting millstones from the rocks of those caves, just as the Phoenicians had two thousand years before. I remember an old man bent over his work, tracing the circular shape of a millstone on a rock. He was holding a compass made from a branch arched by a string—the same kind of compass Punic and Roman artisans had used. More than anything, I remember the beauty of the straits that separate two continents and join a sea with an ocean. The morning sun and evening moon rise in the east over the Mediterranean, and follow their courses to set in the west over the Atlantic.

And then there was the city of Tangier itself. Through my students at the Ibn-el-Khatib secondary school, I discovered the poverty of the Moroccan people. The country's poverty and its natural beauty were, in fact, the two ties that bound me to Morocco from the very first. But there was also hope, and a burning desire to learn. We set up free tutoring services at school: French one night, math or Arabic the next. The textbooks we used had been given to us in France. Yes, hopes were high.

In 1965, everything fell apart. That was the year schools were ordered to deny students the right to repeat a grade more than once if they failed. The poorest were the most severely affected. In March, the army opened fire in the streets of Casablanca, massacring children demonstrating in protest. In October of the same year, the leader of the opposition, Mehdi Ben Barka, was kidnapped in the heart of Paris and never seen again. And so vanished the hope that had been born at the dawn of the country's independence. But the ties I felt were already strong. I loved the country so dearly, there was no way I could ever leave it.

And yet, leave it I did. I had no choice. I was forced to go, deported in 1976 as a foreigner. And that destroyed something inside me.

꿍

I had met Abraham Serfaty four years earlier, in March of 1972. A friend of mine had come over, and we were having dinner together when he asked:

"Would you be willing to hide a Moroccan intellectual wanted by the police?"

"Who?"

"Abraham Serfaty . . ."

All he told me was his name. It was the name of a man I'd never heard of before. But one thing I had heard of was the methods the Moroccan police used at the time: kidnapping, torture, and murder. I thought of my father and the German police, of members of the Algerian National Liberation Front and the French police: Yes, of course I was willing.

In 1999, Abraham and I were living in exile in France. On September 30th, we caught a cab in a nearby town and headed for Orly airport, as we'd been instructed to do by phone. We felt isolated—incredibly so—cut off from everyone because of the strict orders to tell no one about our return to Morocco. We couldn't talk about it, or even mention it to each other, so it didn't seem real. And how could we be really sure that things had changed so suddenly?

We were skeptical because our exile status had become more restrictive. Several months earlier, on May 4th, I had been ruthlessly barred entry to Morocco by order of the minister of the interior, Driss Basri. I was immediately put on the return flight back to France, without so much as a word of explanation, and never got to see—even from a distance—the lawyers and friends who had come to meet me at the airport in Rabat. "Do you have your passport? And your return ticket?" That's all I was asked. The next day, I read in the papers that I'd been banned from Morocco since July, 1991. How was I to know? No one had warned me about anything. During a televised interview, King Hassan II had named me the "prime witness" to the secret prison of Tazmamart—which I was. He also said he had informed me "to never set foot here again." But no one had let me know that. And being a citizen of a democratic republic, I had no idea that a mere statement by the king, casually made on TV to journalists during an interview, could be as binding as law without at least being confirmed by Embassy officials ... Besides, the political police at the Casablanca airport had let me enter the country in 1996, after they had a long phone conversation with the minister of the interior. I could only hear parts of what was said, but finally an agent told me: "You can go through, Madame. You see, Morocco is a tolerant country."

Yet on May 4, 1999, I was sent back to France, convinced, like Abraham, that it would be a long time before I'd be allowed to return to Morocco, despite the change in government with Prime Minister Abderrahman Youssoufi. Abraham took it as just one more sign that he'd never be able to go home. His hopes had been dashed so many times. He continued to fight on principle, but no longer believed anything concrete could be achieved, to the point where he said to me: "Listen. We'll keep our requests to return active, of course, but we won't take any more steps . . ." Sometimes he got so exasperated over being in exile, he'd talk about Pitcairn Island, in the middle of the Pacific Ocean, where the mutineers of the *Bounty* had taken refuge. The island was so small, it didn't appear on any maps and, as a result, escaped the notice of the British fleet. It was a place that seemed to come out of nowhere, outside the realm of the known world, beyond even the very notion of exile. Abraham would say: "That's where we should go live . . ." But getting to Pitcairn Island wasn't that easy.

Then, out of the blue, we had an appointment for 5:30 on September 30th. We knew the time and place, but had no idea who we were supposed to meet. We only had two contacts — an unofficial contact whose code name was "the king's friend" and whose real identity we still didn't know, and an official contact, André Azoulay, one of the king's advisors — but both of them had been called back to Rabat.

The summer of '99 had been filled with hope and anguish — a summer of highly charged emotions, to say the least. We were living in a small village in eastern France (we had moved there in the spring of 1997 because Abraham had wanted to get out of Paris). On July 14th, we saw King Hassan II on television as France's official guest. His health was failing. Even though it was probably intended as a farewell ceremony, I was still surprised that we — the French people and our elected leaders — had invited him to celebrate the anniversary of the storming of the Bastille. After all, that historic event symbolized the fall of arbitrary royal authority. I was also surprised that the king's private guard was marching in the parade instead of the Moroccan army, which had actively participated in both world wars. And I was especially surprised that Hassan II was seated in the same spot where Louis XVI had been guillotined. It struck me as tactless, or—more accurately—in bad taste.

Hassan II died nine days later, on July 23, 1999. Moroccan television broadcast verses from the Koran nonstop before officially announcing his death. We watched the funeral ceremony on TV, then the enthronement of Hassan's eldest son, Mohammed VI. We were so captivated by the images and the news reports that we hadn't really fully grasped the radical change that was taking place before our eyes. Yes, a page had finally been turned. A new king was reigning in Morocco.

And then the reporters and journalists descended on Abraham and me, invading our tiny house in France and monopolizing our time.

In the days that followed, three people took on enormous importance in our lives: Abbes Bouderka, Mehdi Qotbi, and André Azoulay. Abbes Bouderka was a loyal friend of Morocco's Prime Minister, Abderrahman Youssoufi, who represented the USFP (Union Socialiste des Forces Populaires/ People's Socialist Union). I'd known him for a long time and trusted him implicitly. Like me, he couldn't resign himself to the fact that Abraham might die in exile. He discussed the situation with Mehdi Qotbi—a friend of the king—whom he saw from time to time. Mehdi Qotbi was a calligraphic artist. He was living in France, but I had never met him. Abbes didn't reveal Qotbi's name to me until the very last moment.

Ironically, I had a huge blue poster covered with Arabic letters in my bedroom. I had bought it years before at the Arab World Institute in Paris, without even knowing it was by Qotbi. He came from a family of very modest means and was self-taught. He was apolitical, lively, and talkative. And he possessed another extraordinary gift: the ability to communicate. For years, he'd been setting up colloquia, meetings, and trips to Morocco for journalists. He knew everyone there was to know. He founded the Franco-Moroccan Friendship Club (Cercle d'amitié franco-marocaine) and is its current president.

Obliging by nature, Mehdi Qotbi agreed to speak to the new king, Mohammed VI, about Abraham's plight, as Abbes Bouderka had asked. On August 4th, while I was on my way to Geneva for the Sub-Commission on Human Rights, I ran into Abbes in Paris. He gave me the news, still referring to Qotbi as "the king's friend" and not revealing his name. I hadn't said anything about it to Abraham. I was afraid to. His hopes had been crushed so often that the slightest emotion would bring back all the anguish and frustration.

Two weeks later, Abbes called me at home in France. The king had agreed and had even shown concern for logistics: After being away for so long, did Abraham have any relatives in Morocco who could offer him a place to stay? There was one stipulation, however: absolute silence. Not a word was to be said about Abraham's return. It wasn't difficult to understand why that was so important.

At that point, I finally decided to talk to Abraham about the plans.

In September, the king's advisor, André Azoulay, arrived in Paris. He'd been sent by the king himself. He met with

Abraham privately, then with both of us. I'd never seen the man before. He was discreet, easy-going, and efficient. He seemed happy about what he was doing for Abraham. It was André Azoulay who informed Abraham that he was going to be able to return to Morocco.

Abbes initiated the process of Abraham's return, Mehdi Qotbi was the messenger, and André Azoulay the official envoy in charge of carrying it out. But the desire to change things—the decision itself—came from the new king.

ও

Abraham's notoriety was due to the militants in Morocco, France, and Europe who spoke of him ceaselessly. They were the ones who publicized his writings and demanded his rights for him. Without them, nothing would have happened, because no one would have known anything about him or the injustices he'd suffered. As is always the case in situations such as this, the obstinacy and relentlessness of the authorities who opposed him ironically served to make him all the more popular.

By now, Abraham knew he was going to go back to his homeland with "no negotiations necessary or conditions imposed." He just had to wait it out a few more days and keep quiet about it.

Wait . . . We'd waited so long. Fifteen months of hiding, seventeen years in prison, eight years in exile. Waiting. More waiting. Nothing but waiting. Wait for the king to make an official visit to Paris. Wait for the president of France to go to Morocco. Wait for a speech by the king, a pardon, a religious or national holiday; wait for a rumor to become a reality. Wait for life to pass, with death at the end . . . It was a word I couldn't stand seeing or hearing anymore. People live and die in the here and now, today, without waiting. It's in the here and now that they're adults and ready for life. If not now, never.

In Tazmamart prison, they had waited too. Half the inmates died waiting. And what a death it was . . . But I'll talk about Tazmamart later.

ဢ

Now we were on our way to Orly Airport just outside Paris. Abraham was wearing a light-colored suit he'd bought the year before for a return trip that never materialized. He appeared calm, serene. I decided that when the taxi stopped for gas, I'd phone Abbes. I needed to talk to someone who knew what was going on, and could confirm that there really was a meeting set up for 5:30 in the parking lot of the airport Hilton. When I reached him, he said: "I should tell you the name of the king's friend now, because you'll be seeing him soon . . ." That's when the name was revealed to me: Mehdi Qotbi. I'd been under the impression he was connected with the minister of the interior, Driss Basri—an influential political figure radically opposed to letting Abraham return. I didn't say anything in the cab. I decided to wait till we got to the airport.

There were five or six people expecting us at Orly: the Moroccan ambassador and consul general to France, the airport manager of in-transit flights, and some top officials from the French Ministry of the Interior. We all waited together as the passengers boarded the Royal Air Maroc jet. No one was supposed to know before takeoff that Abraham Serfaty was returning home. A communiqué from the royal palace would be issued once the plane was in the air. The tickets they gave us had no names on them, and we weren't on the passenger list. I had disconnected the answering machine at home . . . We were no longer anywhere. When all the passengers had boarded, we headed for the plane without going through security and customs checkpoints. They drove us across the runways up to the aircraft, then carried Abraham on board in his wheelchair to the first-class section up front. The plane took off immediately.

We were seated side by side, holding hands, saying nothing in the unreality of the moment against the darkening sky. Below us was Spain, then the straits, then Tangier, where so many memories converged: the children when they were little, the beauty of the beaches, the merging colors of the ocean and sea; but also the long winter rains, the pupils soaking wet in the cold classrooms, the extreme poverty. Some of them came from Beni-Makada, the poorest part of the city. Two of those former pupils and their wives have remained my dearest friends to this day. One is a professor at the University of Rabat, and the other a taxi driver in Brussels. Tangier isn't a vacation city to me, but rather a mixture of all these things: beauty, squalor, hope. And when I left it, the luminous hope of independence had already died.

Out of habit, I looked out the window to try to see Kenitra and the prison there, as I always did when I flew to Africa — the other Africa: Nouakchott and Dakar. Kenitra prison no longer held Abraham captive. He was now beside me. And when the plane touched down in Rabat, I looked at him and thought to myself that it had been twenty-six years since he'd been a free man in Morocco—a quarter of a century. At last, he and Morocco were going to come to know each other, and I was so lucky to be witnessing the event.

The plane door opened. A young man came on board, smiling broadly, and announced: "I'm Fouad Ali El Himma, head of the royal cabinet. Welcome . . ." The words echoed in my mind. The world had turned around. Eight years earlier, in 1991, Abraham had left from that same airport for his journey in the opposite direction, to begin his exile.

Abraham was quickly taken to the gangway in his wheelchair. I followed behind. It was only later that I saw the scene on television and in the papers. The shot of Abraham smiling as he exited the plane was on every TV screen. Later, a friend told me: "I was overcome with emotion. It was as moving as witnessing the birth of a child." My daughter had been told beforehand, so she was watching too: "I knew it was you, I recognized your legs." Omar Azziman, the minister of justice and a long-time friend, greeted us. He kissed me on the cheeks. Hassan Aourid, the palace spokesman, was there as well, along with André Azoulay, the king's advisor. There was also another man I didn't recognize, who turned and said to me: "I'm Mehdi Qotbi . . ." I kissed him on the cheeks and expressed my thanks.

As planned, the communiqué had been issued by the royal palace during our flight, and the news spread quickly. A crowd of lawyers, friends, and reporters was already waiting at the airport. We got into a limousine, and Abraham said a few words to the people who'd made it past the barricades. Then the car sped off. It was dark, so we couldn't see much and didn't know where we were headed.

They took us to the Hilton. The hotel manager and the head of hotel security were there to greet Abraham, as was a doctor sent by the king. Two cottage suites near the edge of the grounds behind the pool had been reserved for us. Meanwhile, everyone who'd been at the airport had come to the Hilton and descended on the reception desk. But the hotel was full, so there was no way all those people determined to see Abraham could be let in. It was a small mob, and tension was mounting. A friend turned and jokingly told us he was witnessing the only leftist demonstration ever to take place in front of the Hilton. Finally, the hotel made arrangements to open a conference room for the friends and activists who had come. Amid cheers and applause, Abraham talked about his return to Morocco, and why it had been necessary to keep it a secret. I suddenly realized that they were cheering the homecoming of a Moroccan Jew. They hadn't been ordered to do it. There were no slogans prepared. It was all spontaneous. And I was amazed.

I stood in the dimly lit hallway near the entrance to the conference room. So many people came to kiss me on the cheeks and say: "Welcome home!" Friends I hadn't seen since prison, and others I didn't really recognize and whose names I couldn't remember. The mood was warm and enthusiastic. I kept hearing "Welcome home!" and everyone seemed happy.

Later, when we were back in our cottage, I told Abraham: "You couldn't have wished for a better homecoming. You represent the first real sign of change in Morocco."

But this was a new Morocco—a Morocco I didn't know. What points of reference were left for me? In my mind, the real and the imaginary had become entwined. I'd spent my first fourteen years in Morocco in the cities of Tangier and

Casablanca, but it was in the city of Rabat that I spent the second phase of my Moroccan experience, visiting prisons and confronting the police. From March 1986 to July 1991, the Agdal district of Rabat had been my neighborhood. I used to take walks sometimes in the quiet wooded area surrounding the Hilton. And on that 30th of September, 1999, there I was at the very hotel I'd never set foot in before.

In January of 1986, Danielle Mitterand, wife of the president of France, had written to King Hassan II to ask him to let me return to Morocco to marry Abraham Serfaty—in jail. He was serving a life sentence, and his case was gaining attention. As is the policy in many prisons, only family members were allowed to visit. Since he and I weren't related, getting married was the only way we could ever see each other again —the only way I could enter Kenitra, the long-term prison where the entire group of activists had been incarcerated ever since their trial in 1977, nearly ten years earlier.

As a result, I returned to Morocco in March of 1986. When I got off the plane the evening I arrived in Rabat, a white-haired couple—tall and dignified—was waiting for me. It was Jo and Jeannette. Jo, a doctor and one of Abraham's political allies, was a faithful friend. He visited his "cousin" Abraham in prison regularly, accompanied by Jeannette, who would bring her knitting along. In Morocco, where all men are brothers, no one bothered to check whether or not Jo was really Abraham's cousin. Actually, Jo was from the same family—the same political family, that is—an old comrade from the communist party. That night in 1986, Jo and Jeannette took me to their home, a little house in the Agdal district. I lived there for six years. I went to Kenitra four days a week, and spent my evenings and three remaining days with Jo and Jeannette. We got along as if we had always known each other.

No matter where I walked or drove in those days, I was tailed by the police. As a result, a lot of people avoided me, or didn't dare invite me to their homes (I remember the only place to escape police harassment in those days was in prison, under the protection of politicians and the watchful eye of the guards). But in their simple-hearted innocence, Jo and Jeannette were as happy to see me as I was to see them. They were courageous without even knowing it. They gave me everything: the shelter of their home, protection, affection. As the saying goes, fortune favors fools—and those with a good heart: Jo and Jeannette never had any trouble . . . Now they're in France, close to their children. Their house is gone —replaced by an apartment building. The only thing that remained of them in the Rabat I saw that September of '99 was their memory—their absence—as I began the third phase of my Moroccan experience, flooded with recollections of the past. They were the ones I was thinking about in that unfamiliar hotel.

As I looked at Abraham, I could see that, beyond the fatigue and emotion, he was happy at last. And I told him so: "You're happy now, and my work is done . . ."

But was everything that tied me to this country really finished?

ℰ

Three days. We stayed at the Hilton three days. As guests. Some wondered about that and asked if it bothered me. But I thought of Abraham: fifteen months in Casablanca's torture center (Derb Moulay Cherif), seventeen years in prison in Kenitra, eight years in exile in France. Three days at the Hilton. No, it didn't bother me. As for Abraham, he didn't give it a second thought. He'd been told to say nothing until the communiqué announced his return. He had kept quiet and come back to his homeland. Where he slept the first night—in luxury and comfort, or in modest or even stark surroundings —mattered little to him. The important thing was that he was sleeping in Morocco. He has a terrific memory for facts and dates, yet never bears a grudge and rarely dwells on his own scarred past. He's a man who looks to the future with confidence, optimism, and sometimes naiveté, almost like a child.

Our cottage was far from the reception desk. From the edge of the grounds, beyond the pool, a constant flow of visitors could be seen. They came in small groups, and sometimes arrived very early in the morning—as did Hedi, the young son of Abraham's best friend, who died some years ago. The visits extended late into the evening. Friends, activists, Prime Minister Abderrahman Youssoufi, other cabinet members, a government minister who was editor-in-chief of a newspaper, friends from Abraham's younger days, former colleagues from the mining office, and loyal supporters like his cousin— his real cousin—and his cousin's wife, who used to visit him in prison. "How sad it would be if no one had come," I said to Abraham.

And then, the survivors of Tazmamart prison arrived, some traveling great distances to greet Abraham and to see me. For so many years, their names were aligned in columns on lists where we checked off the dead as time went on.

Theirs were the names that appeared in secret letters, penned in minuscule handwriting scribbled on tiny pieces of paper. Tragic letters, letters of desperation . . . Those names were now living human beings by my side—some frail and fragile, like old children. I remember the last letter I received. I turned it over to *Libération,* and the newspaper published it in France. It contained two lists: one of the dead, the other of the dying. The survivors here now were on that second list. I could barely speak. I could only look at them and listen. They were taking me back into the past.

୧

Around thirty years ago, two military coups shook the Moroccan monarchy: one in 1971 and another in 1972. The first took place at Skhirat, the royal oceanfront summer palace where Hassan 11 was celebrating his birthday. There was an abundance of sumptuous food and drink, as well as many invited guests, some of whom had made the trip from Europe especially for the occasion. Suddenly, the Moroccan army's finest—cadets from the Ahermoumou Military Academy in the Middle Atlas Mountains, led by their superiors and under their orders—entered the royal gardens, invaded the palace and the swimming pool area, and killed a large number of people. King Hassan 11 escaped without injury and, with the help of General Oufkir, took hold of the situation. The following summer, on August 16, 1972, while making its way back from Paris, the royal jet was pursued by Moroccan military aircraft. Once again, the king narrowly escaped death. General Oufkir, accused of treason, lost his life.

As a result of the two assassination attempts, the Moroccan army lost its generals: they were all summarily executed. Commissioned and noncommissioned officers were tried and handed prison sentences ranging from eighteen months to twenty years. They were sent to Kenitra, but mysteriously disappeared in August 1973, when they were taken away under the cover of night and transferred to an unknown location. "We don't know anything," was the only information given to family members who went to visit. One evening in 1980, two men rang the bell of the apartment on the twenty-fifth floor of a high-rise where I was living with my youngest daughter, Lucile. The men had a brother among the prisoners who had disappeared. They knew he'd been taken to a secret prison in a small southeastern Moroccan village called Tazmamart. Before they left, they gave me smuggled letters they'd received, recounting the most atrocious conditions: hunger, cold, filth, cells in total darkness day and night. Cells from which no one was ever released, where no visitors came, only the guards—and death, of course, which each prisoner could hear in the other cells as he imagined his own fate. And there was the feeling of abandonment, of not existing. The most awful of feelings. No one talked about them anywhere, except their families—and only in muffled voices. When their prison terms expired, they still weren't released, and the silence continued. One day, a man I've never seen since set up an appointment with me in a café. "Do you want to know where they are?" he asked. "Then look at this . . ." He sketched a map: roads, paths, mountains. "There. Tazmamart. That's where it is."

When the Tazmamart survivors left the Hilton, Abraham turned to me and said, "You saved their lives." But I thought to myself, "I let half of them die." In the course of those ten years, thirty-one of them died a horrible death. I don't want to hear about waiting and being patient anymore. So many have paid with their lives.

How things had suddenly changed! There I was in Rabat. I could see the Tazmamart survivors. I could talk to them. On August 18th, Mohammed VI set up a commission to compensate victims of arbitrary detention. It won't erase the past, but it will help them have a life. Start over . . . Indeed, the change has been spectacular. And so swift. A man at the Hilton came up to me and said: "I'm with the royal security division and have been assigned to protect you. I want to let you know how happy I am that your husband is back home. I'm happy about the change—for you, of course, but for myself and my children as well, for the future of the country . . ."

Could it be possible? The past had been so hard. Was I going to be able to break free of it? Was the time finally over when I had to be on the lookout for agents spying on me, watch them in my rearview mirror as they ran red lights so they wouldn't lose me? And men trailing me everywhere, to the market, to the beach . . . Had all that come to an end? I remember one day in the Habous business district, a merchant whispered to me: "Careful, someone's following you. Watch your purse . . ." Then, with two other men, he walked up to the agent tailing me and started threatening him. Were the days over when I had to avoid checking bags on flights for fear that someone might slip compromising documents or drugs into them, or take documents out that I'd packed? Was I going to be free of that tight feeling in my stomach every time I arrived at an airport, afraid they'd confiscate all my books, detain me for hours in an isolated room, tell my friends

I wasn't on the passenger list, frisk me, question me? Was that part of my past over?

᧡

The day after we arrived in Rabat, Abraham was interviewed on 2M, the second major TV station in Morocco. It was via that television interview that the country got to meet him. He was at his best: natural, extremely upbeat, and full of emotion. Now it was Abraham's turn to become acquainted with the Morocco of today. I didn't see the program. There were too many people around and too many phone calls. But as I walked past the TV screen now and then, I could see Mohammed vi with his brother, Prince Rachid, following close behind. The king's pace was quick. He looked serious and determined—very determined—as he pushed his way through the crowd cheering him. His face was suddenly brightened by a smile as he shook hands and kissed babies, paying no attention to the security guards. This young man is obviously well-liked. Because he's king, of course, but also because he's a different kind of king. Above all, because of who he is. Everywhere, you could hear people saying: "Before, we used to be afraid of the king. Now we're afraid for him." That's a real change . . . Quick: that's the impression the new king gives. Quick in the way he moves, the sports he plays without all the protocol, the decisions he makes, the trips he plans. Yes, quick. Before, everything was so slow. You had to wait. Wait forever. But the new king is moving forward.

We left the Hilton on October 4th.

❧ *The House on the Beach*

A winding path led us to a charming blue and white house on the beach—the kind I'd always dreamed of. It was the vacation home of a friend, Nourredine Ayouch, and he was letting us use it. His wife, Khadija, was waiting for us with some of our closest friends. As tradition dictates, she welcomed us with milk and dates. Hakima Himmish and her husband, Mohammed, were there, as was Mao Fredj (who had been with us every second since we landed) and our longtime friends Abderrahim Berrada and his wife, Monique. Abderrahim is our lawyer. The house had been readied for us. The refrigerator was stocked. There were blankets, towels, a phone, and a TV. The sand and sea were just beyond the garden. It was wonderful—everything Abraham loved. It was a joyous moment, a moment of pure friendship.

❧

I mentioned earlier that my two bonds with Morocco, formed so long ago, had been the beauty of the country and its poverty — the unjust poverty of my students, the difficulties they encountered as they struggled to quench their thirst for knowledge. Poverty at home, all around them, everywhere. Since then, a third bond has become evident to me: the strong ties of friendship I rediscovered and have felt since our return, those friends from whom I'd been separated by the dark years of exile. Hakima, Marie-Louise, Nourredine, Mao, Ghalid, and Anne — all these names, each in its own way, personify struggle, devotion, and a bond of friendship that I could never do without. Over the past thirty years, Abderrahim and Monique have been like an extension of our family, a chosen brother and sister.

ᗕ

What happened to that time in my life when people avoided me . . . and I'd try to rationalize it by thinking that they really did like me, but that they were afraid? In my mind's eye, I can see the faces of the women who hadn't been afraid, but who weren't there at the beach house: my dear Palestinian friend Leila, and my three friends who were employed, one after the other, at the French Embassy. They used to invite me over, then drive me home, only to be followed by the agents trailing me . . .

Between appointments and interviews, Abraham spent some very happy moments at the far edge of the tiny garden, looking at the ocean in front of him. I think he would have loved to go for a swim.

ᗕ

We left for Casablanca on Saturday, October 9th. A welcome rally was scheduled at the cultural center in the district of Maarif. The place was so packed that there were even people standing outside. Arrangements had been made for me to sit on the platform with the others. I couldn't recognize any faces because the light was too dim. One speaker followed another, and there was a great deal of applauding and slogan shouting. Abdellatif Zeroual's father was there. Abdellatif was a young philosopher I'd known quite well. He and Abraham had been close friends. Like Abraham, he had to go into hiding. He was later arrested, and he died under torture in November of 1974, without having divulged anything. His father was frail but extremely dignified. Wearing traditional attire, he was the very image of the poet's description: "dressed in guileless integrity and white linen."[3] I had testified to his son's death at the time it happened. While Abdellatif's father was speaking at the podium, he mentioned me and asked the audience to stand and applaud. I was very touched. And embarrassed.

❦

Eight years had passed since the day Abraham had been called into the warden's office at Kenitra prison. Several people were gathered there. "You're being released," announced a lawyer sent by King Hassan II. They whisked Abraham out, wearing nothing but a pair of jeans and a blue short-sleeved shirt. They didn't let him go back to the cellblock to say goodbye to his fellow inmates or even get his things. "We'll make sure

3. Translators' note: The author is referring to Victor Hugo's poem, "Booz endormi," which figures in the collection *La Légende des siècles*.

you get them. Your cousin will stop by for them this after-noon . . ." After a while in the car, Abraham recognized the route they were taking. It was the road to the airport in Rabat. There was a plane waiting for him. Once it had taken off, the minister of the interior, Driss Basri, made the announcement, and it was picked up by all the networks. In France, phone calls and the news report had tipped us off, so we were able to rush over to Orly just in time to see him arrive. That was in September of 1991. (It was the exact opposite of what happened on September 30, 1999.) A welcome rally had been organized for Abraham at the Mutualité auditorium in Paris. I can still see it. My children were there, as well as my grandchildren, Sara and Denis, running in every direction and coming up to the platform to see me.

ઝ

Christophe, Lise, and Lucile weren't there with me at the rally that October day in Casablanca. They were working in France. My grandchildren, including the youngest, Pablo and Leo, weren't there either. I miss my children. They were all either born or raised here in Morocco, and so they are also deeply attached to this country. Yes, I miss them—and always will in this land where they spent their childhood, and which holds the memories of those times. The story I'm writing is for them, too.

The rally came to an end. I was still onstage and had started looking around for an exit. I wanted to find an inconspicuous way out, but everyone was crowding around. I was being hugged and kissed from every direction. And then, the most unexpected thing happened. It was a miracle. Standing there next to me was Abdelmagid, a former student of mine from many years past at the Oqba-Ben-Nafih secondary school, where I was working in 1975. Back then, I wasn't being interrogated or kept under house arrest anymore. Instead, they just confiscated my passport and followed me everywhere, day and night. I was substitute teaching in the schools on the outskirts of Casablanca. If I remember correctly, it was still winter. The chimneys of the Lafarge cement works were visible from the schoolyard. They served as a landmark to situate the Derb Moulay Cherif police headquarters, where Abraham and his comrades were being held. Derb Moulay Cherif: so many militants were interrogated and tortured there. Dying, Abdellatif Zeroual had been carried out of that prison in a blanket and, under the name of Bakkali, admitted to a hospital, where he succumbed, supposedly to "pulmonary inundation." I'd been taken to Derb Moulay Cherif one night, but I wasn't blindfolded. I could see the road and surrounding area. I saw the secret police offices, hidden at the rear of the official police station. Later, I found my way back to the spot and took pictures of it. Another day, in the summer of 1975, I went up to the guard on duty in the shade cast by the low trees and told him I wanted to see the chief of police. He was so taken aback by my audacity that he let me onto the grounds. Police Chief Yousfi Kadour spoke to me. I was outside in the sun, and he was in the shadows, behind the bars of his office. No, he had no idea who I was talking about. But in any case, they weren't there anymore ...

Never in my wildest dreams could I have hoped to find Abdelmagid again among Casablanca's three million inhabitants. He was just an adolescent when I'd known him. I could only remember his first name. He used to live in the shanty-town of Ben M'sik. One day, I said to him: "I'd like to meet your family and see Ben M'sik." He took me to the shack where he lived. In those days, fires frequently ravaged the shanty-towns. It was believed that speculators who wanted the land set them to force the people to leave. Abdelmagid's little sister had trouble sleeping at night because she was afraid of the flames she kept seeing in her dreams . . . I remember the town was so old—it dated back to the French Protectorate—that there were trees growing between the cardboard and the sheet metal of the shacks.

Twenty-four years had gone by since then. Some of Abdelma-gid's hair had turned white. He'd done time in prison. No, his parents no longer lived in the shantytown. His sister had never married and was living with them. Maybe she still had that fear in her heart. Maybe the fear grew along with her . . .

October 9th wasn't over, and neither were the powerful emotions of the day. The men who had suffered through the great Casablanca trial of 1977 had been planning a reunion dinner for a long time, and it was to take place on October 9th in Mohammedia—where we ultimately settled—about fifteen miles outside Casablanca and forty-five miles from Rabat.

The 1977 Casablanca trial had been intended to set an example, and was open to the public and the press, as well as to lawyers from other countries. It was likewise intended to instill fear. The court revealed itself to be totally servile. The police had been given orders and were sitting near the bench, pulling the strings. The accused were radical opponents of the regime, but none had ever resorted to violence. In all, prison terms totaling three thousand years were handed out. Abraham and four of his comrades were sentenced to life. The principal charge was "conspiring against the internal security of the state." Additionally, it was implied that some of the accused had sided against the outright "reclaiming" of the area of the Sahara that had recently been de-colonized by Spain, and subsequently divided between Morocco and Mauritania. You could intimate it but not say it, because there was—and still is—national unanimity on the issue according to official lines of thinking.

❧

The comrades of the Casablanca trial had organized their reunion dinner down to the last detail, but there was no way they could have foreseen that Abraham would be there, in Morocco, in Mohammedia . . . Who could have imagined it? What an evening it was! All those men who'd been labeled as criminals, traitors, and common law prisoners—I'd seen them so often in the visiting room at the jail. After their release, they'd been rejected, scorned, tagged as ex-convicts. Now, there they all were in that fishing port restaurant, impeccably dressed, with their elegant wives and, in some cases, their grown children. And among themselves, were there any signs of differences, conflicts, bitter words, or resentment? Not at all. Nothing but the dignity of each and every one of them, and the memory of Kenitra, the dark years that had consumed their youth—a time in their lives when they should have been thinking about falling in love, earning a degree, and having children. What had remained in them all was life— shattered, but rebuilt—and the immense joy of seeing each other again. I deeply believe that those men are a blessing to their children, a gift to their country. They are the salt of the earth . . .

The survivors of Tazmamart prison sometimes say they only feel right when they're among themselves—together with others who, like themselves, spent eighteen years buried alive; shared the same suffering, anguish, and indignation, endlessly awaiting death. I understand what they mean. I have a very special bond of confidence and friendship with all those prisoners, as if they provide me with a sense of security and protection. They were the freest of men in this subjugated country because, in everything they confronted, in everything they endured, their thoughts remained free. Being the freest of men, how could they help but reassure those on the outside?

Abraham and I are linked by much the same bond.

I remember being so harassed by the police that I was always afraid I wouldn't make it to the prison: a short taxi ride in Rabat, a long one to get to Kenitra, and another short one up to the prison gates. I had to wait at the entrance, then cross the courtyards as the political police spied on my every move from behind, watching for the tiniest slip-up, looking for any excuse. And maybe they'd find it. I felt totally alone and vulnerable until the door opened. It was a huge metal door. The paint had been worn off by so many hands knocking on the same spot for so long. Then finally, finally, the prison, inside the prison, the maximum security Alif wing where they kept political prisoners. That was where I felt protected, safe . . .

Awhile back, I was in Maarif doing my shopping, and I stopped by the cultural center where a meeting was going on—a "Forum for Truth and Justice" attended by everyone who'd been jailed during those years of repression. I was in a hurry. I had things to do and a train to catch. But after I entered the room, I ended up staying. Everybody was speaking Arabic. I didn't understand much of what was being said, but I knew all the people and felt comfortable. Better than I did outside. Peaceful and safe, as I had felt in the visiting room of the prison's Alif wing.

One day, Jaouad's family invited us to their home. They're practically our neighbors. The men are all ex-political prisoners; it was a cordial evening. Suddenly, I heard a voice that sounded familiar. It was my own! Everyone was laughing. Our friends had found a recording of an interview I'd done with Daniel Mermet back in 1990 for the program *Là-bas si j'y suis* (Over there if you can find me). He was asking me about repression in Morocco. Past and present were more intertwined in my mind than ever.

ઉ

Abraham still didn't have his papers, and we were supposed to leave for France in a few days to get his things. One evening before we were scheduled to depart, three black limousines drove up the narrow road leading to our house on the water. It was the king's advisor (André Azoulay), the head of the royal cabinet (Fouad Ali El Himma), and the *wali* of Rabat (the head of the administrative division). The *wali* presented Abraham with his national identity card and his passport. They had also come to inform us that the king had "put a house at our disposal" in Mohammedia, right nearby, and that

Abraham would be collecting a retirement pension commensurate with his maximum entitlement had he reached his full career potential.

Like so many things, all this was happening so quickly. We'd barely been back in Morocco a month.

That official visit was intended to advise us of important decisions made on our behalf, but it suddenly took on a warm and friendly tone. It turned out that the *wali* of Rabat, Mohammed Guedira, had been working at the phosphate mining office thirty years earlier, at the time Abraham had written the letter urging all company engineers to support the striking miners. That letter ultimately got Abraham fired. The *wali* not only remembered the incident, but knew passages of the letter by heart and recited them for us off the top of his head!

Several days before that, I'd flown to France alone to give a lecture. When I showed my passport to the police officer on duty at the airport in Casablanca, he thumbed through it and said in a troubled tone: "How did you get into the country? Your passport wasn't stamped . . ." He was right. The night we arrived, on September 30th, no one looked at our papers. Besides, Abraham didn't even have any. I tried to explain, as a knot started forming in my stomach. I don't like airports and passport checks. The officer looked at me and then realized the situation, because of what he'd seen on television. He, too, was trying to get his bearings. Before, dealings between me and people in his position were much more clearcut. He apologized, ran to check with his supervisor, and came back to apologize again. Things were moving too quickly for us. He and I were still living in the "before" phase. It was true; the king was moving ahead of us all . . .

When Abraham and I returned to Morocco on November 12th, we found out that the king had dismissed Driss Basri, the minister of the interior, and named Ahmed Midaoui to take his place. At the same time, he appointed Fouad Ali El Himma secretary of state. We were told that the country had exploded with joy at the news. Not long after, the king decorated Driss Basri for service to the royal throne. The move was scarcely challenged. But when Prime Minister Abderrahman Youssoufi arranged a reception to thank Basri for services rendered to the nation, there was a general outcry: demonstrations, questions aimed at the government, press articles calling for the prime minister's resignation . . . Later, it was revealed that some members of the government had refused the invitation, while others had pulled the curtains shut in their cars so as not to be seen . . .

Basri's departure accelerated the return of the political exiles who—like Abraham—hadn't benefited from the royal amnesty of 1994. Among our friends who returned was Hamid, back home in Meknes for the first time. Before going back to Limoges, France, he gave us a call. His voice was choked with emotion. Then our friend Hassan came back with his wife and three children after thirty years in exile to spend "three days in paradise," as he put it when he called me from the airport in Geneva. But the most poignant event for me and many others was the return of Mehdi Ben Barka's family. Many of us gathered at their family home near Rabat. Food was served from dawn well into the night. I had a hard time getting my bearings. The fact that Bashir Ben Barka's wife was there totally confused me. I'd just seen her in Belfort, France, not too long before, and now she was sitting next to Ghita's mother, who has always lived here in Morocco, but whom I'd never met. For once, a Moroccan house wasn't big enough to suit the occasion, so a large tent had been set up. But even that could barely accommodate all the activists, some of whom were quite prestigious. As usual, Ghita and her four children were unpretentious, caring, and attentive to their guests. Bashir told us that earlier that day, he'd had no trouble finding his way to the school he used to attend, even though he was only nine when he'd left Rabat.

There we were, all gathered together. But someone was missing. There was an absence, like a black hole in the universe—those concentrated masses that suck up their own light and remain a mystery forever. I had the impression that everyone there only accentuated the void left by that absent person and, by the same token, the depth of the mystery.

Out in the garden, two little girls romped and frolicked. They were Mehdi Ben Barka's grand-daughters.

❧ Travels Across the Morocco of Today

Night had already fallen when we were taken to see the house the government was providing for us. It was guarded, and was located nearby in a kind of resort community right on the ocean. The first floor was still being prepared for Abraham. Everything would be on one level, just for him. The house was very large, not in terms of the number of rooms, but rather their size. The kitchen was in the basement, separate from everything else and surrounded by empty rooms. I had no idea what they were supposed to be used for, but I was informed that they were for the domestic servants . . . The main rooms were furnished. There were Moroccan banquettes, armchairs in various styles, and chandeliers throughout, but no worktable to put the computer on. They promised to get one for us. Abraham was extremely happy, but I felt a bit lost.

That's where we've been living ever since. As usual in Morocco, the house is cold during the three months of winter, even though the outside temperature never drops below fifty degrees Fahrenheit and usually hovers at around sixty-four or sixty-five. That's because there's generally no insulation, and it's very damp; the heating units are insufficient for such spacious areas. The house is surrounded by a narrow garden. The building takes up almost the entire lot; that's standard here. Large rooms are needed to accommodate family and friends, so the foundation walls are built as far out as possible. The sea view was cut off by hibiscus hedges and the garden wall. We could hear the waves, but couldn't see them.

Abraham loves the ocean, so he had a three-and-a-half-foot section of the hedges cut—no more than that—just enough to allow him to see the water from the veranda. That's all he needed after seventeen years with only a patch of sky to look at, blocked off by prison walls and watchtowers. Just about every day, toward late afternoon when the sun begins to set, he leaves the walled residence to be near the waves. He watches them for a long time, until the sun goes down. Back in October of 1974, when I told him about his sister Evelyne's death, he asked me to drive him to the ocean. He stayed there alone for a long while, sitting on a rock, looking at the water in the light of the setting sun. At the time, he was in hiding. It seems strange now to remember him walking without crutches.

My thoughts are turning to Kenitra and the red evening light. At six o'clock, the guards would clap their hands to announce that visiting hours were over. Then we—the women—would start to file out. The inmates accompanied us to the threshold, but came to an abrupt stop in front of the wideopen door as if an invisible line forbade them from going any further. We went off into the red glow, asking ourselves: "Why? Why do we have to leave them here? And how much longer . . . ?"

Today, Abraham's fondest wish is to be on the sand, get into the water, take a swim, and even navigate an inflatable boat around the bay. And I believe he'll do it.

୧

He gets so many invitations, he has to pick and choose. One of the first things he did was go to Jebel Aouam to talk with the miners in the Middle Atlas Mountains who had been on a long and difficult strike. He also went to Al-Hoceima, a small town on the northern coast, then to Larache. It gave him a chance to see the country, become familiar with it once again, find out what it's like today. I wasn't able to go with him.

I did accompany him to Tetuan, though. It's a charming, sleepy little town, similar to what you find in Andalusia. I'd come to know it when I lived in Tangier and often went to the beach at Martil or Oued Laou, a few miles from there. I remember watching the long black fishing boats glide along, as they were pulled in from the blue water onto the blond sand. But my most beautiful memories, the ones I'm most fond of, take me back to M'dik—a long beach on the Mediterranean where we used to camp on the deserted sands. That's where Lucile said her first words when she was a baby.

I didn't recognize Martil. With all the new buildings, it had become an extension of Tetuan. Nor did I recognize the new part of Tetuan that has been built up over the last twenty years. I decided not to visit Oued Laou or M'dik, because I didn't want to destroy my memory of them. Everybody has his or her own Morocco. I've been told that the most popular spot in M'dik now is Cabo Negro, where the country's rich spend their summers. The sand must be covered with money. And perhaps the sea as well . . . Who knows?

They gave us a wonderfully warm welcome in Tetuan. Dozens and dozens of activists and members of various associations had organized a cultural event for Sunday afternoon. And of course, there were several speakers. It was a good show, and the speeches were kept short. When it was over, a black cloth screen was unrolled on the stage. Everyone who'd taken part in the day's activities came up and painted something on it in white, as a souvenir of their participation. Little by little, the screen got brighter—just like the future of this country—until all the darkness was gone.

While I was there, I ran into Amina and her husband, Doctor Jaidi. They are now and forever part of what anchors me to this country and to life. Dr. Jaidi spent six years in prison. During that time, Amina cared for their two young children on her meager salary as a public service psychiatrist. She used to make the trip from Tetuan to Tangier to visit her husband, then go back home the same day. During the whole ordeal, she had to fight the administration, the police, and all the absurdity that went along with it. People at the event would say to me: "Oh, yes; I remember. We fought for them . . ." But that's wrong: they're the ones who fought for us.

The North used to be the Spanish zone, at once feared and hated by the French Protectorate. It was the territory of the rebels led by Abd el-Krim during the Rif War (1920–26), and later the scene of the 1958 revolt that was so brutally repressed the following year. For forty years, it was rejected, neglected, and unloved by the Moroccan monarchy. Desperately poor, the North is the point of departure for people emigrating to urban areas, especially in Europe. It's synonymous with smuggled goods from Spanish enclaves—the presidios of Ceuta and Melilla. It's also synonymous with *"pateras"*—the boats overloaded with young people who risk death, and sometimes find it in the turbulent waters of the straits, in their quest for a better life. And, of course, the North means drugs. The marijuana growing out in the open there is a source of income for the peasants who cultivate it, and it brings in much more money—astronomical sums—for drug dealers, who make little effort to conceal their activities. They drive Mercedes, build apartments and villas, then launder the rest of the money and get it out of the country.

A few years ago, while visiting jails in Spain, I asked, as I always do, to talk with foreign prisoners. Knowing if they want to stay or would rather go back to their own countries helps me assess the conditions of the jails where they're being held. I believe it was in Seville that all of them told me they wanted to stay. All but one: a Moroccan. I was shocked. Didn't he know what Moroccan jails were like? I've never forgotten his expression of surprise, contempt, and haughtiness as he looked me up and down: "Me? In prison in Morocco? I'd be out of there in less than an hour. My car and all my friends would be waiting for me . . ." He was a drug lord.

Interestingly, the North is also a gateway to the world, to Europe. It has strong ties with Spain, whose coast is visible from all points, and whose lights can be seen shining in the night. The Spanish television stations that everyone watches here have continuously provided extensive coverage of the country's move toward modernization, its transition to democracy, and its regionalization efforts. Paradoxically, smuggling and drugs have also supported a host of small-income operations and tightened the social fabric, limiting social splintering and rifts, and causing a very uneven redistribution of wealth. And yet, although the development of the North has been neglected, although its economy is totally unorganized and left to all types of trafficking, its human resources are considerable. You can see and feel that. How can we repair these wrongs and clean up the mess? Mohammed VI appears to have understood the need for positive action. Since assuming power, he has visited the North twice, expressing the monarchy's renewed interest in the region, and the importance of change. He was cheered and welcomed everywhere he went. The interest the king has shown, the gesture he has made on two occasions, could very well be the beginning of a viable reunification of the North and South, which has consistently and tragically failed ever since Morocco gained its independence.

A week later, in early December, we were in Marrakesh, at the invitation of activists there. Since Abraham and I returned to Morocco, I'd already been to Marrakesh with Anne, my friend from Geneva. I love Marrakesh and the surrounding region for a number of reasons that are intertwined in my heart and mind. I've often hiked in the mountains there, in winter and spring alike. And the memory of those times is superimposed on others from my childhood. My father was a mountain climber; it was his passion. Loving the mountains is a special kind of love that only those who've experienced it can understand. Who doesn't like the ocean, blue water, sun and sand? Everyone loves the ocean. Mountains are another matter. They were our love. As children, my younger brother and I would always be on the lookout for the first glimpse of snow on the summits as we drew near the mountains. Whoever spotted it was the winner . . . The snow in the distance, against the blue sky, was the first sign of the joys awaiting us. Even today, I try to spot the Atlas Mountains. Seeing the immense, white-capped mountain chain against the blue sky, over the palm trees, takes me back to my childhood and is a promise of happiness.

I've often hiked in the mountains: in the snows of Oukaï-meden, the little Moroccan ski resort; around Imlil through villages that seem suspended between the peaks and valleys, at the foot of Toubkal, the highest point of the Atlas Mountains. I've hiked through the pebbled plains that lead down to the desert, in search of prehistoric remains; in the *wadi,* dried water beds, to gather pieces of coralline from between the stones; and especially on the Yagour plateau that juts out over the plains of Marrakesh and is so green in the spring. It's a magical place—truly magical—an ancient place of worship: in pre-historic times, shepherds came to pray at the base of a pyramid-shaped mountain there. Hidden in the grass, a flat stone with etchings on it serves as evidence of their presence and fervor. Among the etchings is a tiny outline of a man lying there. It's naively executed, but very moving . . .

I missed all of that so intensely that I wrote a novel whose story takes place in the midst of those mountains. It was in recreating the world I loved so much that I was able to vicariously live there once again.

ري

Ramadan had just begun. We were invited to a *ftor,* the meal at sunset marking the end of the day's fasting. They served the wonderful traditional soup, *harira*, followed by white soup prepared with milk and semolina, then dates and cakes soaked in honey. There were around fifty people there in total, all part of Marrakesh's high society, according to a friend of mine. And it was obvious from their refinement and tact. All the city's democratically minded citizens were present, and Abraham was very happy: he's a man who has always wanted to unite people, get them together, get beyond sectarianism. That's true now more than ever, because he wants to better understand each and every aspect of a Morocco that has been transformed.

We were next to our friends—Fatima and her husband, Ahmed Abadarine—who had arranged the evening. They're human rights activists who are just as sincere and courageous in their commitments as they are in their daily lives. They stand tall and straight.

They put us up in a guest cottage, where friends came by and prepared an impromptu dinner. In the morning, I went out into the garden. We were in the Targa district of Marrakesh. There was an abundance of orange trees, and the Atlas Mountains were looming in the background, capped with snow. The sun's brightness made everything glisten—the dark leaves of the shrubs, the palms, the air itself.

Not far from there, General Oufkir's children spent the final years of their wretched captivity in very limited comfort. Following the general's death in 1972, his wife and six children vanished. The youngest of the children was two and a half at the time. Not many people in France—and no one in Morocco—dared talk about them. Oufkir was a highly charged name. Some thought of him as the man who tried to assassinate the king; others considered him the regime's strong man during those long years of political repression and instability, a man with many deaths on his conscience — activists arrested by his agents, peasants in the Rif area, rioters in Casablanca, maybe even Mehdi Ben Barka. In his time — 1962 — he had had Abraham arrested.

But what about Oufkir's children? All we could do in France was call attention to their plight and publicly question their disappearance. Not much else. In 1987, four of them managed to escape from the secret prison where they were being held. They went on foot, knocking at the doors of former friends for shelter. They made it all the way to Tangier, where they put out a plea for help on the radio. During their tragic getaway, few people would have anything to do with them, including the French administrative staff of Medi 1 radio. Some lawyers in France were moved to action by the incidents — among them, Bernard Dortevel, who went to Morocco to meet with the Oufkirs. They spoke at length. Naturally, the Oufkirs were taken into custody again, but the incident caused such a scandal that the conditions of their detention were improved: they were transferred to a house in the Targa area of Marrakesh, where members of the family and lawyers were allowed to visit them under tight surveillance.

When I used to go to the visiting room in Kenitra, I'd sit beside a young woman who, through a series of roundabout links, got news about the Oufkirs. She'd mumble what she knew to me under her breath, and I'd carry the news to France each time I went back. The woman was afraid, even there in the visiting room in Kenitra. In those days, we were all afraid.

૭

The next day, Abraham and I attended another ceremony. This one was in commemoration of the death of Saïda Menehbi, a young activist who died while on a hunger strike in 1977. It was the first time a public gathering to honor the memory of those who perished during the years of repression was allowed. Before, such events had taken place in homes among family members. The hall was full, and there was a big crowd outside. Saïda's mother and the mother of another young hunger strike victim, Bel Houari, who died in 1984, were seated side by side on the platform. I remembered that many more would have died if Professor Minkowski hadn't agreed to intervene at the last minute. He was able to exert tremendous pressure because of his reputation.

Speakers addressed the audience one after the other. Then it was Abraham's turn. While he was talking, several rows of young people in the hall would stand up in unison, feverishly shouting slogans, then sit down again. They continued shouting and demonstrating out into the street.

Before leaving Marrakesh, Abraham and his friends went to take a look at the city's newer neighborhoods. The buildings were shabby and overcrowded; that was where newcomers to the city came to live. I went to the medina and into the souks, where nothing had changed—except that the beggars and young Moroccans who used to harass tourists were gone. Special squads had been assigned to prevent them from frightening the tourists away. What were all those young people doing now? And where were all the beggars who used to hang around Jemaa-el-Fna Square?

It's impossible to go beyond Marrakesh by train. It's the end of the line. The only way to go any further is by car or on foot. The city is pressed up against a mountain; on the other side is a huge desert. Marrakesh is a dead end, a trap. Nothing comes from the south—no resources, no information. There's no portal to attract people or minds. Moroccans know very little about Africa. They hate the desert and obstinately turn their back on it. What could they expect from its deadly aridness, a potential indication of their own—they who consider anything green to be beautiful? What could they expect from its nomads transformed into "mercenaries" for the Polisario, from a covert war everyone refuses to recognize, interrupted by a cease-fire that hasn't brought peace?

The mountain subsists, just barely, because of family solidarity and money sent back home by emigrants. Little by little, it's being drained. Marrakesh lives off tourism, depends on it; but where are all the profits going? They're being redistributed poorly, if at all. The social gap is palpable, and that's what essentially drives people to extremes.

We didn't go to see the palm groves. They've been desecrated by construction projects. It's said that half the trees have been cut down. It breaks my heart to watch the country's natural heritage disappear as the years go by, whether it's the palm groves of Marrakesh or the beautiful lagoon of Oualidia.

Abraham can't travel by train, because there are no accommodations for the handicapped. The degenerative condition affecting his legs forces him to use a wheelchair. Somebody drove us home. On the way back, I could tell Abraham really wanted to drive, but he would have needed an assistive device with hand brakes next to the steering wheel.

ઉ

The month of Ramadan was slowly coming to an end, and so was the year. We decided to spend New Year's Eve here in Morocco. And we spent it alone, together. People who wanted to break with the austerity of Ramadan went to Europe to party. Others, ourselves included, stayed home and watched the millennium celebrations around the world on TV. New Year's festivities aren't really popular here. They're dampened by discrepancies regarding times and dates. There is great tolerance in this Islamic country for the "people of the book" — as Jews and Christians are called here — and that facilitates combining calendars and dates. Naturally, public life — the century and millennium — is determined by the Christian calendar. But on that night, everyone here knew that it was really the last week of Ramadan in the year 1420 of the Hegira — it was written in all the Arabic newspapers. Everything was rather mixed up, even the time of day. Although we are in the same time zone as Europe, Morocco observes "universal time," as the radio and TV stations call it. So on the eve of the millennium, when it was midnight in Europe, it was only 11 P.M. here. But Abraham and I cheated a bit and raised our glasses, in keeping with European time.

December 31, 1999. Now it was midnight in Morocco too — midnight universal time . . . The foghorns of the boats hailed the arrival of the year 2000. We may have even heard the boat horns in the port of Casablanca, faintly audible in the distance beyond those of Mohammedia. It was hard to tell because of the *chergui*, an easterly wind that blows everything away from us, including sound. Abraham said to me in the darkness: "I haven't heard them at midnight on New Year's Eve since 1975. I was at Derb Moulay Cherif then, and it was hard . . ."

The only thing we could hear after that was the pounding of the waves on the beach.

Ever since he came back to Morocco, memories have been resurfacing in Abraham's mind—or rather, he's begun to talk about them. He's protected, shielded by his return, wrapped up in the country he's rediscovering. He's protected from himself, from the difficult past, from the fifteen months he spent in Casablanca's secret detention center whose name he spoke out loud that night: Derb Moulay Cherif, where they bound his feet, handcuffed him, blindfolded him, made him lie on the ground and not utter a sound, tortured him each time they interrogated him. Yes, it was hard . . . He may be grandiloquent when he addresses the public, but he can take the other extreme in his private life and become laconic, understated, and restrained, if not completely silent—as he was on that New Year's Eve.

December 31, 1999. Morocco was repenting. The 31st was the deadline the Compensation Commission had set for submitting requests. That evening, activists gathered for a candlelight sit-in, demanding that the deadline be extended. It was staged in the heart of Rabat, where throngs passed by on that night of Ramadan, which was also the eve of the turn of the century.

December 31, 1999. The royal palace announced that the king had named a new secretary general to the Ministry of the Interior. He'd also named eight *walis* (regional administrators with broad powers) and twenty-three provincial governors. Their appointment to the high positions they were to occupy was done unceremoniously. They would assume their functions without the pomp and circumstance that dated from another era, without having to prostrate themselves or go through the traditional hand-kissing and public oath-taking, as used to be the case. One month earlier, the head of the DST (Direction de la Surveillance du Territoire: Morocco's counter-intelligence agency) had been replaced. It was essentially a dismantling of the entire "Basri system," with the exception of its most covert elements.

Nothing's changing here?

On December 21st, the Arabic-language daily printed by the OADP (Organisation de L'Action Démocratique Populaire) began publishing a serialized version of the book I'd written in 1992 entitled *Tazmamart: Une prison de la mort au Maroc* (Tazmamart: A Death Prison in Morocco). It had originally been published by Éditions Stock in Paris, and had been banned in Morocco. The newspaper announced the serial on the front page and included a picture of the book's cover: a National Geographic Institute map with a tiny dot showing Tazmamart, circled in red to highlight it . . .

Nothing's changing?

I don't know where this country is headed. Honestly, I really have no idea at all; but it's moving very quickly to break from its past—to escape it perhaps . . . And it's the royal palace that's leading the way.

❧ How Do We Deal with the Past?

The fact that the ceremony in Casablanca which commemorated the torture-induced deaths of Abdellatif Zeroual and Amine Tahani took place in public marked another first. With so many people attending, emotions ran high. Amine Tahani's wife was in the audience, and her teenage son read a speech from the podium. He was shy but focused. Abdellatif Zeroual's entire family was there as well. We hugged and kissed when it was over.

On my way out, I picked up a brochure lying on a table and thumbed through it. On the last page was a long list of names. In front of each was the crime the man had supposedly committed and been tried for during the years of repression. Of course, no explanations whatsoever were given, not one iota of evidence produced to support the accusations. I thought to myself that in a lawful country, the individuals who drew up and distributed a list like that would be tried themselves—and probably found guilty. People who've been living under a lawless government for so long are totally uncultivated themselves. They have no notion of what "lawfulness" is. I noticed the name of a dead man on the list.

How can we find out who was responsible for the atrocities committed during those years of repression? How do we deal with them? In fact, how do we deal with the past: a past that includes yesterday but has a forty-year history behind it, whose victims are here with us today and walk by their persecutors in the streets? How do we deal with a past that has swept up victims and persecutors alike? Their traces fade in the sands of forgetfulness, because no one has dared speak out, because no charges were ever laid — no investigations ever conducted.

It's an open debate among friends, within human rights organizations, and in the papers, but it's a purely Moroccan one that doesn't take into account the rest of the world and its experiences. The humanist John Donne, who so long ago wrote: "never send to know for whom the bell tolls; It tolls for thee," also said that no one is an island isolated from the continent. Yet all of Morocco is truly cut off, isolated on the north by the Mediterranean, on the west by the Atlantic, on the south by an enormous desert plagued by war, and on the east by a long border that has remained closed for decades. On top of all that, Moroccans are cut off mentally by their strong feelings of identity and nationalism. They form an island, just like the Chinese must have during the Middle Empire. They're convinced of their uniqueness, or at the very least of the uniqueness of both their misfortunes and windfalls. Travel and symposia have made little or no difference, because the inner wall that isolates Morocco's thirty million inhabitants from the rest of the world is so thick. It's an ancient wall, built to resist foreign invaders—from the early Portuguese and Turks right up to the more recent Spanish and French colonizers. In order to drive them back, the country closed itself off militarily as best it could; but more importantly, it strengthened its own identity, cultivating a special kind of density as a means of fending off any new input from the vast world outside . . .

Something of that remains to this day, despite Western customs. The issue of minority languages is perceived here as a national problem, as are the ties between religion and the monarchy, the democratization process, transition, regional development, the legal system, and, incidentally, the past. But by and large, sub-Saharan Africa, Latin America, pre–and post–World War II Europe, and all absolute monarchies the world over have experienced similar problems.

Moroccans don't know that. They're just now beginning to find out. They don't know that African countries have multiple languages—in some cases dozens of them—or that Asian countries each have different alphabets and ideograms. They're not aware that every absolute monarchy, from time immemorial, has been tied to a single religion, or strives to be. In a word, they don't realize that all these debates have already taken place somewhere else and in other eras.

That's something that also permeates the banalities of everyday life in Morocco. One day, when I was with friends, the conversation turned to how cold the houses are here and how hot it gets in the summer. I casually mentioned that there was no comparison with the African continent's really suffocating heat in places like Mali, Niger, and Djibouti . . . Everyone looked at me in surprise: "Have you experienced it?"

"Yes, I have." But everybody had already started talking over me all at once, claiming there was nothing like the heat in Marrakesh or Ouarzazate, or anywhere else in Morocco for that matter . . . I give up. The rest of the world doesn't exist. There's nowhere but Morocco.

Whether they admit it or not, and no matter how much they love Morocco, foreigners get the feeling now and then that the country's closed off, that it's far removed from the planet's crossroads of communication. But at the same time, that very isolation gives Morocco's internal debates an intensity and freshness that have sometimes been lost elsewhere.

Foreigners . . . There lies one of the country's greatest contradictions. On the one hand, Moroccan hospitality is legendary. Guests are honored, welcomed, well received. It's a tradition Moroccans are all proud of. But on the other hand, in political discourse, the word "foreign" resonates like an insult, almost a kind of betrayal, and is used to designate anything originating outside Morocco's borders: the atmosphere that reigns in Morocco is one of ultra-nationalism, of a nation at war, threatened on all sides. Yet it's been almost half a century now since the country became independent. Lyautey is long gone. Even his statue has been taken down and tucked away in the French Consulate's gardens. The principal border dispute concerns the western Sahara, and has pitted Polisario Saharawis, Morocco, and, by extension, Algeria against each other since 1975. Above and beyond the United Nations referendum, dialogue must take place among us, so that together we can attempt to resolve the vital problems of the Maghreb.

ဢ

Every time we visit friends or attend a meeting, every time I read an article in the Moroccan newspapers, I encounter points of view so different from my own that I have to reevaluate my position. Human rights organizations express, proclaim, and demand it all: truth, justice, reconciliation, and an international court for crimes against humanity. The Compensation Commission created by the king on August 18, 1999, is at the heart of every discussion. It's definitely inadequate. Some of its members have shady pasts, or reputations for being irresolute, and there seems to be no room for appeal once it makes a decision. Some favor boycotting it and recommend that people not file any requests; others say they should go ahead and file because it's a way of starting a paper trail. Rumor has it that three thousand—maybe even five thousand requests have already been made.

Those who are heatedly discussing the issue make little or no distinction between "arbitrary detention" and "unfair trials." But the Compensation Commission has only focused on victims of arbitrary detention. That stance automatically excludes everyone who was sentenced as the result of a trial, regardless of whether or not the trial had been fair. And during those years of repression, who wasn't judged unfairly? The Forum for Truth and Justice, comprising everyone victimized during that dark period, has entered into dialogue with the Commission's leaders. Its mandate will be broadened. We're in a period of transition, I'm told: we need to look squarely at tomorrow, devote all our energy to building the future, ensure the success of the changes in progress. We should not look back at the past.

I understand that. Of course I do. Yet how can we rid ourselves of the past?

Air Force Sergeant Rachdi Ben Aïssa was a nice young man who had no idea of the plotting that was going on in August of 1972. He was completely innocent, yet he was tried and sentenced to three years in prison. He ended up spending fifteen years in Tazmamart, where he finally died. He was extremely skilled with his hands, the most skilled of anyone in Building One. He could make a needle out of a metal shard, pierce an eye in it, and thread it in the black night of Tazmamart. He drew a sketch of himself on a scrap of paper, a kind of self-portrait, showing a small figure with long, unkempt hair, quietly seated on the stone ledge. He measured everything—the length, width, height, even the air holes of his tomblike cell—and noted the dimensions in the margin of his drawing.

Rachdi Ben Aïssa died in 1988. As he was dying, he said: "I want my drawing to make it out of here," as if by releasing the picture to the world, he would, in a way, gain his own freedom. His drawing did make it out and was shown more than once on television. The U.N.'s High Commissioner for Human Rights made sure that it was displayed for all visitors to see at the Hall of Nations in Geneva. At least that's something . . .

When I think about Rachdi Ben Aïssa, I cease to understand. I don't want to understand.

Who are the guilty ones? Who was responsible? Who benefited at the top of the chain of command? Who amassed shameful fortunes, not wanting to know the truth, or knew but kept silent? When I think about Rachdi Ben Aïssa's drawing, all I can see are guilty faces, including my own: guilty for not having been able to prevent what happened.

A friend of ours who is a scientist and university professor believes that it's imperative for Morocco's future to set up a committee composed of enlightened individuals who might succeed in bringing victims and persecutors together. That would be one way of getting to the bottom of the truth once and for all, opening the way to the serenity of forgiveness. He's right; I think we should. I believe it's necessary. But what a difficult task it would be! Where would we find those "enlightened individuals"? Where would we find our own Desmond Tutu? How can we identify the real persecutors, accomplices, cowards, and swindlers in the tangle of Moroccan society? At least in South Africa, the racism of apartheid, horrible as it was, produced a preliminary sorting out. Here in Morocco, we need to start from scratch. The guards in Tazmamart were military personnel, as were those in the chain of command, and the monarch is the commander-in-chief of the army. Among the military personnel were some who felt pity: they provided the prisoners with writing tools; carried letters to their families; brought the prisoners medicine, news from the outside, money — a portion of which the prisoners gave back to them. The smuggled letters addressed to the prisoners' families would read: "Give him the money. He'll keep half, and the rest will go for things here in prison." Thanks to the military personnel who were sympathetic to them, the prisoners were able to get radio parts from the souk, so they could put together makeshift transistors and hear that people on the outside were talking about their plight. If it hadn't been for those guards, all the prisoners would have died. A few families received news of their loved ones from guards on military leave. But in many instances, the news wasn't spread to other families, because of personal grudges or sheer spite. As a result, some families got no news at all . . .

Not everyone on the side of the persecutors was ruthless. And not all the victims were generous and good.

෧

Abraham is a man who looks to the future, just as his gaze is now poised on the open sea. He's a man who is not consumed by bitterness or the need to seek revenge. As many do—as I do—he believes in the necessity of truth and only wants one thing: that the main perpetrators be ousted from politics and public life. Nothing more? No, nothing more. The not-so-distant past cannot be called into question in its entirety, either in terms of moral responsibility (because that would necessitate going too high up the ranks and destabilizing the very foundations of religious authority) or in terms of politics (because too many people who are still useful or even essential today—people who defend the transition—would be put in jeopardy or would oppose it).

For now, it would be enough of a change if you didn't run into torturers in front of the U.N. Committee against Torture in Geneva, as was the case a few years ago; if they no longer headed political parties, as is the case today; if they didn't lend their support to the establishment of human rights organizations; if high-ranking officials from those years of repression and lawlessness were barred from teaching law in Moroccan universities.

෨

And while I'm at it, let's put an end in everyone's mind to the very notion of impunity. A large segment of society was corrupt to the core. It still is, and will be for a long time, until it dies out. It needs to be contained, kept from doing more harm. It needs to be pushed aside one day, weakened, and perhaps forced to invest usefully in this country. That's all many Moroccans are asking. That the power to harm be taken away from those people. The people of Morocco are still whispering: "In the past, we used to be afraid of the king. Now we're afraid for him."

We're going through a transition. Let's hope it's successful.

❧ The Long Road to Democracy

After spending so many years in Morocco, I finally got to see Rabat's Mechouar from the inside. A friend of mine who works at the Primature, the prime minister's offices, drove me through. It's an immense walled area, containing a number of buildings: private villas reserved for palace personnel, the Primature, the Ministry of Habous[4] and Islamic Affairs, the royal college off to one side, the great mosque, and of course the royal palace itself—an enormous white-walled, green-tiled building whose layout looks extremely complex. That's the first thing you notice: a heavy, massive palace with a dense and intricate shape, both stiff and angular. The ambassadors' gate was closed, as was the golden gate, shining in the sunlight, that had opened in July of 1999 to let Hassan II's coffin pass through. That's the gate the king uses when he goes to the Ahl-Fas mosque in the Mechouar on

4. Translators' note: The Ministry of Habous is the government division overseeing funds and capital-generating income earmarked for the maintenance and upkeep of religious institutions: mosques, Koranic schools, holy Islamic sites, etc.

horseback, under the shade of a parasol. Within the compound, there's a great deal of unused space, and the placement of the buildings gives the impression of having been left to chance.

When I mentioned that to some friends, they protested: "On the contrary, nothing here is ever left to chance." "Ritual determines every detail concerning the Commander of the Faithful," they affirmed with an air of grandeur. "That's the Moroccan way . . ." I didn't say anything, of course, but I thought to myself: More rules and protocol than at the courts of Philip II of Spain, Maria Theresa of Austria, or Louis XIV of France? I doubt that. Protocol may vary from country to country, but it's through protocol that kings the world over set the distance between themselves and their naive, awe-struck subjects.

In his daily life, Morocco's new young king doesn't always burden himself with formality. In contrast to his father, he doesn't live in the palace, but rather in his own house just outside the city—where he was living when he was crown prince. He drives himself to work at the palace every day, without a motorcade. His bodyguards are in another car. I'm even told he stops for red lights.

§

I've been reading the Moroccan Constitution. It was adopted by referendum on September 13, 1993, and revised in 1996:

"Morocco shall have a democratic, social, and constitutional monarchy."

"Social." We won't bother talking about that aspect, because it's still a total failure nearly half a century after Morocco became an independent country.

"Constitutional." Yes, because there's a constitution.

"Democratic?" In this country, democracy is defined by only two criteria: the separation of powers and the multiparty system. Who could argue to the contrary? Those are indeed two of the criteria used to judge any political system. Yet, while they're essential, they're not enough.

A multiparty system has been in place since the country became independent, and is provided for in article 3 of the Constitution: "There shall be no one-party system." In 1997, when there were two elections (municipal in June and legislative in November), it was even instituted in the system of government as a result of the authorization of requests for the legalization of new parties and the occurrence of splits within existing parties. Examples? The PJD (Party for Justice and Development) led by Dr. Khatib, a former supporter of the national movement opposed to the French Protectorate, opened its ranks that year to Mr. Benkirane's pro-Islamic partisans, thereby gaining nine seats in Parliament. The Moroccan communist party, known as the PPS (Party for Progress and Socialism) lost a number of its members who left to create the FFD (Democratic Forces Front). A split of the OADP (Organization for Democratic and Popular Action) gave rise to the PSD (Social Democratic Party). The scattering of votes that resulted made electoral fraud that much easier—a practice that has been forever present in Morocco.

The separation of powers is guaranteed by the Constitution, as are civil liberties. But of course, in reality it's a different story. For all practical purposes, the judiciary system has no autonomy. Up to now, it has taken orders from the police and the executive branch. But it's in the process of being reformed. Omar Azziman, the country's minister of justice, is quietly spearheading drastic changes. He's one of the four "sovereign ministers," along with the minister of the interior, the minister of defense, and the minister of Habous (religious affairs). "Sovereign ministers" are appointed by the king, and answer directly to him. Omar Azziman is well respected. He's an academic, a law professor in Rabat, and was a founding member of the Moroccan Human Rights Organization in 1988. He was originally named minister of human rights by Hassan II, and subsequently minister of justice. The reforms he's implementing focus on two points: modernization, and rehabilitating and revamping the justice system. Everything is being overhauled: recruitment, training, supervision of magistrates. New approaches to working with the courts are being explored, and information technology is being incorporated — something he believes in quite strongly as a means of ensuring transparency. Following a three-month session, the High Council of the Judiciary finally announced significant changes with respect to the Moroccan magistracy. But all this is taking time — a long time. Too long, claim critics.

Legislature is the responsibility of the parliament, which comprises two houses: the House (or Assembly) of Representatives, whose members are publicly elected, and the House of Councilors, which passes laws. But the Constitution states that "the king shall have the right to deliver addresses to the nation and to the parliament. The messages . . . shall not be subject to any debate." The Constitution gives the king the prerogative to legislate via "*dahirs*" (royal decrees) on specific matters.

At the executive level, a duality of powers clearly exists, which is also expressed in the Constitution. It states that the law (voted on by Parliament) "is the supreme expression of the nation's will," but that the king is "the supreme representative of the nation" and that "the government shall be answerable to the king and the parliament."

The very nature of democracy, as it is defined by the Constitution, remains ambiguous, and is never discussed by the media. It is never debated or analyzed. Nowhere is it stated that in this democracy, the people are sovereign; that it is the people who express their will by universal suffrage; and that the government answers only to the people. The people are totally absent from the Moroccan Constitution. The word appears nowhere. Moroccans exist only as a nation or country. Yet the king always begins his addresses to the nation with "My dear people," and he repeats the phrase several times during his speeches. That means that by the king's own words, Moroccans are at once a people and subjects—I almost wrote "a people of subjects!"

§

Whether they criticize it or support it, Moroccans believe their political system is unconventional, if not unique, because the king is the "Amir Al-Muminin" (the Commander of the Faithful) by virtue of the fact that he is the *sharif;* that is, like so many others in the region, a descendant of the Prophet, who was sent by God and who was the last of the prophets.

They're wrong. All the absolute monarchies of the world, from the pharaohs in Egypt to the kings of France and czars of Russia claimed—and continue to claim—their divine legitimacy. Their subjects have to be believers and, if possible, of the same religion . . . In Morocco, another type of legitimacy has slipped its way in, next to the prince's: the legitimacy of the "nation." But between legitimacy bestowed by God and legitimacy bestowed by humans, it's God's that takes precedence. The motto of the kingdom is: "God, the Country, the King."

୧

I put aside the dry text of the Constitution to look and listen around me. Some claim the Constitution should be changed. Abraham doesn't agree. He thinks the one we have needs to be upheld in its entirety instead; if elections were held today, we'd end up with exactly the same Assembly (of Representatives), or perhaps one that might be even more hesitant and reactionary.

୧

"The right to vote here," someone confided to me, "means the right to choose who'll pay me the most." Some of the young people have been shouting: "Down with the monarchy." "I'm for a republic . . . ," a friend of mine said. People should be allowed to say that in public—just as in a republic, people can claim to be monarchists. The king should reign, but not govern—as in Spain. "In my country," a Spanish friend told me, "the democratization process was like an avalanche. Here in Morocco, it's happening one drop at a time . . ." "Nothing's changed; the Makhzen is still here," maintain the hard-line militants, who realize that all the changes in this country have been initiated by the king. The Makhzen, which is the nucleus of despotic power and brazen wealth, still bears the stigma of decades of oppression.

I'm reminded of the eighteenth century and the enlightened despots, rulers who were friends of the philosophers and who used to say: "Everything for the people; nothing by the people." I wonder if that's where we are now. Is it a stage we have to go through? The king is immensely popular, because he's the king everyone had been waiting for. It's wonderful that Moroccans have a king they can like. For the moment, his popularity protects him from every possible danger. Or does it? It doesn't protect him from organized crime—from those who have amassed fortunes and acquired privileges, and who certainly don't want things to change. But the king's popularity does protect him, for now, from the Islamists— from those who, until the "poor man's king" took the throne, were the only ones to take up the issue of poverty.

In any case, the one thing I'm sure of is that Morocco will be truly democratic when it's possible to shout "Long live the Republic!" with complete freedom, the same way people can shout "Long live the King!" in a republic.

❧

The king . . . In the Tafilalt region in the South, he hugged an old woman and gave her food. In Tangier and Tetuan, he took children in his arms. No matter where he is, he heads into the crowd, heedless of the security agents' warnings. When he receives guests, he lets them shake his hand, if they prefer that to the traditional hand-kissing. He is the hope of this country.

But somebody's got to tell him that official vehicles shouldn't drive over carpets. So I'll be the one. Those carpets are the work of a thousand and one poor, humble hands, the priceless objects of the rural world—so priceless that tradition dictates removing one's shoes before treading on them. To have the beauty of their designs and colors crushed and stained by expensive machines from another world is, in my opinion, a sign of disrespect.

It's a tradition, some say. Moroccans are proud of their carpets, and they want their sovereign to see them. In that case, why not hang them on walls like paintings, or spread them on the ground? But the cars should stop well away from them. Royalty should approach on foot and walk upon their astonishing splendor.

❧ Life Goes On

*A*braham wanted to be with me at my first book signing in Morocco. The owner of the bookstore is a friend of mine, Marie-Louise Belarbi. She's made her shop in Casablanca, Le Carrefour des Livres, exactly what a bookstore should be. It's bustling and lively, and she frequently arranges book signings to give people an opportunity to meet and engage in literary discussions. The book in question was my one and only novel, *La Femme d'Ijoukak* (The Woman from Ijoukak). The story takes place in Morocco. The moderator of the event was the poet and author Salah el Ouadihe, a courageous man who wrote the famous *Lettre à mon tortionnaire* (Letter to My Torturer). He and his brother, Aziz, had both attended the Mohammed v school where I used to teach. He'd also been an inmate at the long-term prison in Kenitra—in the same group as Abraham.

The night before the book signing, I attended a beautiful performance at the French Institute in Casablanca by the singer and poet Malek. It was my first evening out in

Morocco—that is, my first evening out as an "ordinary person." The Institute was the same, yet at the same time had changed quite a bit. It had been modernized and was now open to young people and children, even toddlers. I was with my friend Marie-Louise, who is Malek's mother. The hall was full, and people were standing. I was being stared at, there was no doubt about it. I think people recognized me, but I felt comfortable—as if nothing had happened, as if I'd led a normal life, as if the weight of those dark years had suddenly been lifted. The past had taken a step back to make way for the present . . .

The following evening, there were a lot of people at the bookstore. They had come for the book signing and to meet Abraham, too. The mood was warm and friendly. The night before, at Malek's performance, I was facing the stage. Now, I was looking out at the audience. I could see their faces. Some I recognized, some I'd forgotten; others were new. The blending of past and present was all the more disconcerting because it stemmed from both the people who had come to the bookstore and the neighborhood of Maarif itself, where I'd often done my shopping and whose every street was familiar to me.

Abraham was unable to find the Maarif of his childhood, the Maarif of his days as a young activist with the national movement. The neighborhood had become unrecognizable to him. As we drove through it, he looked around in surprise: Where were all the children who used to play ball? Where was the little house where he'd lived with his sister and parents? I, on the other hand, had been back to the neighborhood several times since our return to Morocco—to the bookstore and shops on the nearby streets. But I hadn't gone back to the market that I knew all too well, because I was caught between the fear of no longer recognizing anyone and the apprehension of seeing people from before, from the past that is no more, that I cannot let go—nor do I want to. The other day in Rabat, for example, I was walking down the *rue* des Consuls when a shopkeeper recognized me. He was very happy and hugged me. Then he gave me one of those copper bowls, the kind I'm so fond of, that bathers in *hammam*s use to pour water over themselves. He remembered I liked them. But what else did he know? What did he know about my long absence?

Abraham was looking for his past, too: his past as an activist, which had begun when he was eighteen . . . Actually, it had begun even earlier, when he took part in a demonstration organized by French Gaullists. They were shouting "Vive la France!" in the streets. He would have loved to have shouted along with them, shouted for joy over the Allied victory and the landing of American troops. But to shout "Vive la France!" under the French Protectorate? Impossible. So instead, he shouted "Long live the Republic!" with all his heart . . . That's how he got involved in activism, and he's never stopped since. He joined the cause the way others join religious orders. It was forever, with his eyes locked on the distant horizon, blind to the shoulders of the road, confident in the progress of humanity, happy to have taken part in it all, and never entertaining the thought that he might have fought in vain.

I've often fought in vain, but I have absolutely no regrets about it . . . What I'd never be able to tolerate would be not having fought at all.

We were invited to meet the local French press—about twenty journalists brought to Morocco by Mehdi Qotbi. It was set to take place in the Tour Hassan Hotel. I hadn't been back there since I'd gone to meet an American friend of mine and her husband ten years earlier. I was being tailed, as usual, but the police didn't know who my friends were, so they had to take pictures of them. Two police agents hid behind newspapers and photographed us nonstop. The clicking sounds of their cameras gave them away, and my American friends had a good laugh over it.

During the luncheon with the journalists, Abraham held a genuine press conference, answering every question put to him. Friends tell us our house must be bugged from top to bottom . . . Maybe, but what for? What we have to say doesn't bother anybody anymore, and we don't engage in doubletalk. Abraham simply told the reporters what he would say anywhere, even at home. The weight of such a recent past is still palpable: many people don't dare speak openly, especially on the phone. Why not? We do. And we talk to the press. So why should anyone bother with bugging devices?

I went on a tour of Rabat with the journalists. I felt comfortable in their company, and would have liked to prolong the pleasure of the moment with a few of them. But these were fleeting encounters. Now my life here is full of fleeting moments. Too fleeting. That's unfortunate . . .

The journalists' bus driver politely offered to drive me to my next appointment. I took him up on it and was the only passenger on the bus as we crossed the city of Rabat. A very young man—almost a child—was seated next to the driver. I asked:

"Is he the grease monkey?"

"Yes, he is . . ."

"Grease monkey." That expression took me back in time. It had slipped out without forethought, but it carried me back to a distant past, to the enchanted days when I was just discovering Morocco and its mountainous terrain. It was a time when drivers and mechanics used to repair the old rattletrap buses right on the side of the road, and passengers had to push the bus up hills, then jump back in, wading through bags and cackling poultry, as it coasted downhill. I owned a Renault 4L and provided free taxi service for a week across the back roads in the South, along with a friend of mine. One day, a passenger pointed to my friend and asked: "Is she the grease monkey?" Yes, she was . . . There are still grease monkeys in Morocco today, even on that fancy bus reserved for members of the French press that crossed Rabat just for me. For me. I had finally returned to Morocco.

៽

"Your picture is in the newspaper," the carpenter told me. "Did you see it? It's in the Arabic-language papers, too. You're famous!" He smiled happily. "Do you happen to have a French copy of your book on Tazmamart? I read parts of it in the Arabic paper, but I'd like to read the whole thing in French . . ." Unfortunately, I didn't. I didn't think I'd be allowed to bring it with me to Morocco. Things had changed so quickly here since the summer of '99 . . .

Moroccans are exploring their past. They want to know the truth about everything. That seems to be the intent of the latest official directives. Yes, the truth about everything—about the people who disappeared: Where? When? How? And especially, Who? And once that's all been revealed, what should be done to the people who were responsible for it? They're everywhere: especially in the secret service, but also in the police force and military. Who can the young king count on for support? And there's the deceased king, Hassan II, and all his deep, dark secrets. But he's dead now, and judging the dead is simply not done. His son, Mohammed VI, can't turn against him, can't denounce his own father, so he's decided to distance himself from his father by actions rather than words.

And as far as I'm concerned, actions do speak louder than words.

ॐ

I took the train at the Agdal station in Rabat to go back home to Mohammedia. Ten years earlier, when I wanted to get the agents who were shadowing me off my trail, I'd go to the train station in downtown Rabat and ask the ticket clerk in a loud voice for a one-way ticket to Casa-Port. When the agent following me heard that, he'd immediately call ahead to tell the others to be waiting for me at Casa-Port. But I'd get off at Rabat-Agdal instead, and be free of them for the rest of the day.

How the train station had changed! The city had grown, and so had the neighborhood. The parking lot was full, and the station itself had been renovated and modernized. People

I didn't know greeted me. I shared a compartment on the train with a man and woman. I had a copy of the French-language, Casablanca-based weekly, *Le Journal.* The headlines read: "Torturer Asks His Victims to Forgive Him." The man snickered: "He could have just not tortured them in the first place; but it's too late for that now . . ." We struck up a conversation. At one point, I mentioned that my husband had been tortured, and said who he was. The man fell silent and looked out the window. I interpreted his reaction as hostility and thought I'd made a mistake in talking about it. We were approaching the Mohammedia station and the train began to slow down. The man got up. He looked solemn and deeply moved. Without saying a word, he shook my hand for a long time. I felt ashamed of myself for what I'd assumed. I was still living in the past, a past when that name—Abraham Serfaty—was blacklisted, when Abraham was attacked from all sides by some and detested by others. I couldn't help recalling the horror of anti-Semitism and racism.

As always, there were a few kids begging for money at the Mohammedia station. I normally don't pay any attention to them, but that day I did. I watched as they went to the grocery store and bought glue, ordinary patch glue. They put it on a rag, inhaled it, and didn't stop till they were high. They were eight years old. Maybe ten.

ॐ

I got a taxi at the station, and the driver picked up another passenger on the way—a student from Niger. Naturally, he was Black, and he was friendly and smiling. He said he was studying law here in Morocco and that it was better than in Niger, because Moroccan degrees were more highly regarded than the ones granted in his country. I asked him: "Are people polite to you?" He smiled and said: "Yes, some are. But there are racists too . . . They're always asking me what time it is, to get me to look at the watch on my arm, and then they laugh at the color of my skin."

The taxi driver was an elderly man. So he wouldn't feel ashamed—and because it's true—I said: "People in France are racist, too. Usually against Moroccans and Algerians." He answered, with a sad look: "In Morocco, they're racist against Africans." I was a coward. I didn't dare mention the Jews to him.

What's the situation regarding anti-Semitism in Morocco? In everyday language, do people still use "Jew" and "Zionist" interchangeably? Yes, all too often they do.

My father, a Protestant layman and the youngest university administrator in France, took the initiative on his own to publicly protest the laws governing the status of Jews decreed by the Vichy government. I was in school at the time, and I knew about the status of Jews. I knew, from that point on, they'd be singled out. And I knew it was a disgrace. I've been told there were adults who were totally unaware of the situation, even in Vichy . . .

Can't anything be done against that here in Morocco? People tell me about the happy, harmonious relations Muslims and Jews had in the past. Abraham says that when his father went to the synagogue, the neighborhood's Muslim merchants would greet him with respect and friendship as he walked by. In Europe, too, the change was barely perceptible in the beginning. The Jews in Germany claimed they'd been totally integrated, and boasted of the good relations they had with non-Jewish Germans. "It can't happen here . . . ," they insisted, much the same way Jews claim it's impossible here, in the "here" where I'm living now. What harm is there in adding "Hachak, with all due respect," after pronouncing the word "Jew"? It's just a popular expression, you might say. And what harm, you might ask, is there in saying "Jew" instead of "Israeli" or "Zionist"? What are such tiny slips of the tongue compared to the Nazi concentration camps? I'm not Jewish. I'm from a Protestant family, but have no religious affiliations; "of Protestant heritage" is what that's called, it seems. Regardless, I do not tolerate racism in any shape or form, whether against Blacks or Jews. When that's at issue, nothing should slip by, ever. It's always in the here and now that we must act.

ᦡ

And there's certainly work to be done in the here and now! In his "Memorandum to Whom It May Concern," Sheik Abdessalam Yassine accused King Hassan II of having expressed "his keen interest in and affection for cosmopolitan Zionism," of having "friends who were of the Jewish faith and Zionist ideology." He also spoke of a "Judeocracy." At the same time, Mr. Rami, a former Moroccan army lieutenant who took refuge in Sweden, gave an interview on the television station Al-Jazeera that broadcasts from the Persian Gulf. Rami was a staunch supporter of Oufkir, and is a racist fundamentalist with ties to neo-Nazi groups. His remarks during the interview were violently anti-Semitic and aimed at, among others, Abraham and André Azoulay, the king's advisor. To top it off, in Morocco's number one weekly, *Le Journal,* a former Resistance fighter wrote that "all Moroccans are Muslims." What about Moroccan Jews? Don't they count? What about all of them? Have you banished them from your memory because of criticism or scorn, or is this simply due to linguistic and behavioral negligence? Or is it because of the growing confusion between culture, religion, and ideology? Have you forgotten about the Judaized Berbers, who were here long before the Arabs?

What I consider serious — very serious — is that these slips have generated little reaction here. And there's no non-government organization or association in Morocco to fight racism. As in all Arab countries, anti-Semitism exists here. True, it's low-grade, but it's pervasive. And even the best-intentioned people have resigned themselves to the fact that it does exist; it lingers, and goes with the territory. That's a pretty far cry from a democratic or tolerant society. It's pretty far from the basic principle that each and every person's relationship with God is not a matter of state, but rather a personal issue between the individual and his or her conscience. When something has to be imposed by the state, it ceases to have any real value or meaning.

 formula

Abraham used to spend hours on the computer when he was in France. He'd receive and send e-mails, and read the newspapers on the Internet. He was always looking for news about

Morocco. Since he's been back here, he spends less time on the computer. People come to visit; journalists call on him, and he gives interviews. He listens more than he used to. He's reacquainting himself with his country. Words often resound in the living room as various people express their opinions. I only hope the words aren't falling on deaf ears.

The milder the weather gets, the more Abraham is drawn to the ocean. He's tried out a four-wheel dune buggy that can take him right up to the waves. From there, he should actually be able to go into the water one of these days. I always knew he'd work out a way to do it. Here on his home turf, he lets things come to him more, by way of his visitors.

ℭ

Morocco, much more than Europe, is the kingdom of words — spoken words. Everyone's life here takes on a spoken form. Indeed, verbalizing their lives sometimes relieves people of having to act, because once something's been said, it's as good as done. I speak, therefore I am. Now I have a better understanding of the mania here for hidden microphones, and the secret police's obsession with tapping phone conversations — the police of the past, during the years of repression, and maybe even the police of today. I can better understand the gut fear they trigger. It's not just the fear of repression. Words are everything: proof of your existence, a form of identity. So it's terrifying to think that your words can be overheard and appropriated. It deeply shakes an individual's stability, the stability of the society I'm living in now. "Oh come on, Christine darling! Of course you're being wiretapped. Of course they've bugged your house and phone . . ." I don't want to know about it. I want to block my ears, close my eyes, hide my head in the sand. Yes, like an ostrich. I want to live in ignorance of that kind of world, a world lurking in the shadows. If I can't be free—totally liberated from the old police machine—if I can't be certain that I am free of it, then I prefer at least believing that I am.

❧ Women, Islam, and Islamism

"*I*slam shall be the state religion. The state shall guarantee freedom of worship for all." Those are the exact words of the Constitution. Aside from the "Jewish exception" (a Moroccan community which is, in fact, allowed to practice its faith), no other religion can be practiced by Moroccans. You can't be Moroccan and Christian, or Moroccan and Buddhist. Civil legal documents are nonexistent, because the very concept of secularism is absent. The life of every Moroccan, whether Jewish or Muslim, is determined by a religious status called the "personal status." And the Mudawwana (meaning "code" in Arabic) sets forth the particulars of this personal and family law for all Muslims. All the rules that it comprises are religious in nature. Tampering with one of these rules is tantamount to tampering with religion.

❧

These days, the Mudawwana is a word that instills fear in everyone: in women, because it's a reminder of their misfortune; in men, because they're afraid it might be modified in some way. Progressive factions have demanded its modification, calling such action necessary. However, religious leaders oppose it in the name of Islam. During the previous reign, and under the newly-elected government, a bill outlining women's legal rights was drafted in March of 1999. No one seemed to take much interest in it except women, who had begun to mobilize even before then: they established both a support network for the Plan for Action to Integrate Women in Development, and a Front for Moroccan Women's Rights. Despite the differing views held by their members, the two movements decided to merge and work together. They organized an extensive petition campaign, and slowly succeeded in gaining considerable support from associations and the population in general. They actually represent much more than just a band of feminist splinter groups, isolated in an intensely male-chauvinist society. This kind of women's mobilization is a relatively new phenomenon here.

The draft bill, called the National Plan for Action to Integrate Women in Development, was initiated by Saïd Saadi, secretary of state for social, family, and child welfare at the Ministry of Social Development, Solidarity, Employment, and Professional Training. In glancing over a copy of the document on my desk, I saw a number of proposals dealing with women's health, education, and the fight against ignorance and illiteracy. The plan is divided into two phases: the first addresses short-term emergency measures, slated for implementation in the year 2000; the second is aimed at mid-range objectives to be achieved between 1999 and 2003. Literacy initiatives and the fight against ignorance are part of a broad program sponsored by the monarchy and the government: namely, a reform of the educational system intended to eradicate ignorance and illiteracy by 2015. Revamping education is a top national priority (second only to the territorial unity issue), and educational reforms have been presented in Parliament.

The French language newspaper *Libération*, published by the peoples' socialist union (*Union socialiste des forces populaires*), printed a full-page spread outlining the plan's main points. The headline read: "Who could be opposed to this?" I took another look at the proposed bill and, in rereading it, thought to myself: Yes indeed, who could be opposed? And yet . . . Following the eighty-five page text was a five- or six-page document entitled "The Personal Status Code." It was *the* code, the Mudawwana.

෬

In December 1999 and January 2000, opposition forces against women got organized. A Committee for the Defense of the Family was created. Among its backers were some surprising names, sad to say. The PJD (Party for Justice and Development), a supposedly moderate Islamic affiliation, went on the warpath. Under the leadership of Mr. Benkirane and Dr. Khatib, the affiliation decided to form a political party and get seats in Parliament. Various other associations belonging to the amorphous Islamic grouping followed suit. But the Justice and Charity Association headed by the charismatic leader, Sheik Abdessalam Yassine—still under house arrest—kept quiet.

The king clearly expressed his concern for the plight of women, especially in rural areas, in a speech he delivered on August 20th; yet the government remained guarded if not silent on the issue. The proposed bill appears to have been a single-handed initiative by the secretary of state, Saïd Saadi. The minister of Habous and Islamic Affairs, Alaoui M'Daghri, a sovereign minister and therefore answerable only to the king, voiced his total opposition from the very beginning in the name of Islam. In the name of Islam? Perhaps. There are so many ways in the world to live one's religion, so many ways to interpret sacred texts. Yet I can't help but believe that these men feel their privileges are being threatened, and they're seeking to maintain them at whatever cost, even if it means courting madness. In mosques, imams speak of the "debauchery" of women, labeling them as "degenerates" and "alcoholics." They denounce "those who've sold out to the Jews and Christians." Whatever happened to the often-praised tolerance of Muslims toward the "people of the book," toward the Jews and Christians, whose prophets—Abraham, Moses, and Jesus—are all recognized by true Islam?

When Prime Minister Abderrahman Youssoufi addressed Parliament on January 13th, everyone took notice. He supported the Plan for Action to integrate Women in Development, thereby making it a legislative proposal.

❧

But what changes to personal status did the National Plan for Action provide for? Why was it causing so much animosity? Here are the main proposals:

- A concerted effort to prevent early marriages, especially in remote areas, by raising the legal marrying age to eighteen.

- The right for women of legal age to no longer be required to have a "guardian" in order to conclude marriage agreements. Would such a change put an end to the notion — which till now has gone unchallenged — that women here remain minors all their lives?

- Changes in the repudiation procedure leading to divorce. The intent is to grant women the same rights as men. Till now, the law has stipulated that women cannot divorce unless they pay back their own dowry, the value of which is generally haggled over and inflated to the point where the amount makes divorce totally prohibitive. In reality, only men have the right to repudiate.

- The abolition of polygamy. As it stands now, the husband merely needs the consent of his first wife to enter into polygamous relationships.

- A more equitable division of property and possessions in the event of a repudiation, i.e., a fair sharing of goods jointly acquired during the course of the marriage—through an inheritance, for example.

ᶘ

Next came proposed modifications to the Mudawwana concerning the custody of children, remarriage of mothers who have child custody, conjugal residence, legal guardianship of minors, and all the authorizations women must obtain from a father or husband to be able to travel, work, etc.

The Islamists of the PJD suddenly revealed their true colors. Previously, they had limited their activities to charitable work in poor neighborhoods. They had maintained a low profile, to such an extent that many people underestimated their power. Now they were showing themselves for the activists they were, and there were quite a few of them . . . Sheik Abdessalam Yassine's Justice and Charity Association still said nothing, preferring to remain on the sidelines of the conflict.

A friend of mine said: "The Islamists don't have any activists. They just have a clientele." I don't agree. They may have a clientele, but they have activists as well, and are perhaps the only ones who do. They showed up with music and pamphlets at a fair in Casablanca that focused on women in rural areas. They campaign door-to-door, debate wherever and whenever possible, get people in administrative agencies to sign their petitions, "descend" on meetings—to use their own terminology—either arriving before everyone else and dispersing themselves throughout the room to monopolize the discussions and block debate, or literally surrounding the audience with a human chain of militants, thus creating the visual impact of a prison or hostage-taking incident. Leftists don't subscribe to that type of activism anymore. All that remain are their convictions, their group efforts, and the anguish of women in the face of what their future—and the future of their daughters—might be like.

Algeria and Afghanistan come to mind. It is said that discussions with Islamists from those countries frequently take place at the mosque in Maarif, Casablanca. One Friday, at around one o'clock in the afternoon, high prayer was in progress, and the square in front of the mosque was filled with men prostrating themselves on the ground. If the cars that had been momentarily abandoned in the streets in total chaos were any indication, the crowd was not just composed of poor men. "Will they go as far as civil war?" Abraham asked me.

ॐ

True, there have been a number of blunders. For example, Muslim legal specialists weren't consulted in the drafting of the National Plan for Action. No mention of them was made in the introduction or preamble. If they had been included, some of them might have supported the project. But since they weren't, they unanimously opposed it. And why were the indisputable clauses of the plan—nine-tenths of its content—lumped together with the proposed modifications to the Mudawwana? If they really wanted to make headway, shouldn't the Mudawwana have been examined separately, in consultation with Muslim legal specialists?

A few days before the vote, everyone knew the proposed bill would not be adopted. Parliament would reject it. Three parties—the Islamic party and two moderate parties—had already made their positions clear: they would vote against it if no changes were made. Then it was announced that the PPS—the secretary of state's party which had initiated the project—and the Islamic party with representation in Parliament that had opposed the plan had reached an agreement to iron out the problems. Abraham felt that the Left hadn't mobilized enough and that, sadly, stalling was the only alternative.

Then, all of a sudden, everything came to a halt. Morocco lost the soccer match against Nigeria by two points and was eliminated from the Africa Cup. That could affect the country's chances of being a candidate for the 2006 World Cup. It was a national disaster and made the front page of all the papers . . . In the face of such a calamity, what importance could the plight of women have? "Bread and circus," the Romans used to say. Here there's only circus. Where's the bread for the poor?

Bread for the poor . . . Mustapha spends Sundays with his wife and little girl in their one-room apartment in a working-class neighborhood. They go to the big Joutia market in the morning to buy wheat. His wife makes her own bread every day. It tastes better, and it's cheaper. They don't have an oven, so she takes the unbaked dough to the neighborhood's public ovens. Their diet consists mainly of bread dipped in oil or tea. They buy milk for their daughter.

When Mustapha left his father's house after quitting school, he came to Mohammedia with seven *dirham*s in his pocket—about fifty cents: enough to buy some bread and lemonade. But he had no place to sleep. He's been working or looking for work ever since. The monthly minimum wage is 1,600 *dirham*s—a little over $140. Mustapha has rarely had a steady income. He and Aïda married soon after they met. Going against tradition, Aïda's parents accepted the fact that their daughter was marrying a man incapable of paying them a penny of dowry money. All Mustapha could afford was fifteen chickens to serve the forty wedding guests, and three hundred *dirham*s to pay the "*adouls*," Muslim notaries, to draw up the wedding contract. Since the wedding, he's continued doing odd jobs as an unskilled construction laborer or gardener. The work lasts a day or sometimes a week at a time, and once, only once, he remembers having work that lasted a whole month straight . . . He even got a "*carossa*," one of those small rickety push-carts, and tried selling vegetables and oranges, pushing his meager fortune wherever he went. If he got work for a few hours or a couple of days, Aïda would sell the vegetables and oranges in his place. He says she's helped him tremendously.

Now he's working in a private home as a domestic, driving the car, doing the cleaning, and running errands. His salary is above minimum wage, and he's ecstatic. And yet . . . Their rent is six hundred *dirham*s. They have no furniture, no bed or mattress, only blankets they roll up during the day. He just bought the first jacket he's ever owned from a used clothes dealer passing through. It cost forty *dirham*s.

"I want my daughter to go to school," Mustapha told me. "I want her to be like a boy. I don't want any more kids; I want her to get an education." Mustapha only finished the sixth grade. He was an excellent student. He reads Arabic well, is very intelligent, and is interested in everything. He had to quit school because he didn't have the financial resources to continue. He really doesn't regret it though. He feels that if he had continued, he might have a diploma but still no work—due to the constant strikes here.

Once a year, for the Aïd el-Kebir holiday, and sometimes twice a year, Mustapha goes to visit his father, fifteen miles away. He takes a taxi with his wife and daughter. That means there's a fare to be paid for each of them—a big expense for the family. They have to walk the last three and a half miles because the taxi can't take them any further. There's no electricity or telephone at his father's house, but there is a well. The village where he lives isn't way up in some remote mountain area—it's in the province of Ben Slimane, just under twenty-five miles from Casablanca. Mustapha is the oldest of nine children, and his father is always very happy to see him.

Mustapha has no expectations for the future—nothing specific, that is. All he has is a dream: to own a taxi and earn his living with it. But he needs a permit, an "approval." Theoretically, preference is given to former military personnel and to the destitute. The reality is that to obtain an "approval," being destitute isn't enough. You have to know someone highly placed who will pull strings for you, over all the other destitute applicants . . . And then there's the real heart of the problem: how to pay for the taxi. Mustapha knows all that. As I said, he's very smart and has a clear perspective on the precariousness of his existence. He's the oldest of the family; his father is just as poor as he is and has nothing to give him. In this part of the world, poverty, like wealth, is hereditary. The channels for advancement in society have been blocked for a long time. Even college graduates are out of work.

"Include my last name: Zentout . . . ," Mustapha said to me.

"Are you sure?"

"Yes, I want my name to be in your book . . ."

So, I've included his name. And what about his life? There are worse fates, much worse. His is just an ordinary life—the life of a poor man.

ઉ

It hadn't rained for a long time. It rained in the fall, and there was a shower on January 10th, but there had been no more rain since. We wondered if it was going to be a dry year.

ॐ

I wanted to know more about what life was like for un-schooled women coming from poor families in rural areas, so I went to see Aïcha in Casablanca at her Women's Solidarity Association. She explained that she changed the term she uses to designate the women the association helps. Before, they were called "unwed mothers." Then she met some Islamists at the fair in Casablanca and, while talking with them, found out that they interpreted "unwed mother" to mean "prostitute." They accused her of fostering prostitution by protecting such women. From then on, she's been using the term "abandoned mother" instead. In all her years as a social worker, she has only come across two women who chose to have a child out of wedlock, but with a father, a real father for their child. All the others fall into two categories of victims:

- Those who have been physically raped. Within this group is a sub-category of "opaque" cases. That's the word Aïcha uses to refer to incest victims. In a society that so rigidly separates the sexes—where the sexual moral code is so imposing—fathers, brothers, uncles, and cousins are in-tensely attracted to the young women and little girls in the household who are at their disposal every day.

- Those who have been mentally raped, to use Aïcha's terminology. This category includes women who have been repudiated—a nightmare that remains a constant fear for all women—and whose husbands have decided they want to take them back. It seems like salvation, so the women agree. However, they're forgetting that they're no longer "married," but rather "repudiated." They fail to have a new marriage certificate drawn up, or are afraid to ask for one. After a while, sometimes after only a few days, their husbands abandon them a second time, often leaving them pregnant and with their status unchanged: they're still "repudiated." The majority are illiterate and from rural areas.

"Frequently they give birth all alone," said Aïcha, "then kill the baby." At dawn in Casablanca, finding dead newborns is not uncommon. If the women check into a maternity hospital, they have no place to go once they get out, no place except the streets. The only way they can survive is by turning to prostitution . . ." Aïcha comes to their rescue with the Women's Solidarity Association. She welcomes them, but doesn't offer charity. She trains them to be domestics, cooks, or pastry chefs, and gets them jobs. She plans to open a *hammam*, where some of the women will work. A friend brought over an Italian pasta machine so they could learn to make fresh pasta and sell it. Many of the women refuse to work in private homes. They usually started out as domestics around the age of five or six, and ended up being mistreated or raped. Even if they eventually happen upon nice employers, they rarely stay on. The women have already opened a small restaurant with a few tables in the building where the association is located, and they intend to open a pastry shop on the ground floor.

The women rent modest rooms in working-class neighborhoods, where they live with their children. Once they've paid the rent, electricity, and water, there's not much left of their salaries. Domestic help is paid one hundred and forty *dirham*s per week in most households. Each morning, before going to work, they drop their children off at the Women's Solidarity daycare center. When the children turn four or five, they're sent to the neighborhood school so they can have a chance to grow up like other children.

"I'm going to ask Doha to come in so you can talk with her," Aïcha told me. Doha entered the room timidly and smiled as she sat down, like a good little girl. She was twenty-five or twenty-six, and worked in the association's restaurant. She had a five-year-old daughter, Dounia, who was in school. We were seated in an office where two or three people were working, coming and going as they went about their business. Doha barely spoke, answering questions with a simple yes or no. But when we were alone with her, she started to open up. Her voice got louder and she spoke more quickly. With frenzied anguish, she told us about her childhood, her life: how she'd been raped by her uncle when she was a child. She was so little when it happened, she had trouble remembering the details. Her uncle would do horrible things to her while she tended the flock in the field. Doha fell silent. After a moment, she went on to explain how she had tried to talk about it with her mother, who was separated from her father. Her mother had only lived with him two days, just enough time to become pregnant with Doha. Then he repudiated her. Doha was so confused, she didn't know if she was a child or a woman. She no longer knew who she was. She had been raised and breast-fed by her grandmother, who had also raised and breast-fed the uncle who raped her. Was that man her brother or her uncle? And Doha . . . Who was she?

When Doha spoke in a loud, firm voice, she was beautiful, her black eyes sparkling. The violence that had been done to her, the violence she'd had to stifle for so many years, showed in her face and in her gestures. When she first arrived at the association, Aïcha said, she was in bad shape. She had a love-hate relationship with her daughter. She used to beat her, and might have ended up killing her, even though she loved her. She was seen by the psychiatrist who comes to the association on a regular basis, and suddenly one day, she confided in him. At first, she talked about Dounia's father, who didn't want to give his name to his daughter, didn't even want to see her. In Doha's mind, her misfortunes were the result of that child, the daughter she hated and beat, the daughter she loved. And they were the result of all the love she'd never had. She didn't dare go deeper within herself. She couldn't. And then one day, she spoke of her mutilated childhood, of the rape and incest that no one in Morocco wants to admit to, that doesn't exist, according to respectable people . . . Doha was on the verge of a nervous breakdown. Aïcha took her in her arms and calmed her down.

She continued her story. Last year, before the Feast of the Lamb, she tried once again to see Dounia's father to ask him for help. She left her daughter with neighbors. When she returned to the neighbors' house, Dounia was crying. The man had bought a live lamb and brought it back to the house.

His children were shouting with joy. Dounia said to her mother: "I want a daddy who'll bring me a lamb. I want a lamb, even if it's just a little tiny lamb." With her hand, she showed her mother the height of the tiny lamb she wanted — no bigger than a toy. Tears were streaming down Dounia's face. Doha was crying too: for her daughter, Dounia, and for herself, Doha, when she was a child. She was crying for both of them, for their double tragedy. Doha and her daughter were at the Women's Solidarity Association on the day of the feast. Someone had donated a lamb to the association, so Doha and Dounia were able to share in the celebration . . . "I hate all these holidays," Aïcha told me. "Especially the Feast of the Lamb. I really wish the new king would abolish them . . ."

There are lots of Dohas and Dounias in Morocco.

ૐ

There was a rumor circulating: Sheik Abdessalam Yassine had supposedly written a letter to the king. This was followed by a second rumor: "The letter's on the Internet. Do you want to see it?" Yes, I did. I read it.

Sheik Abdessalam Yassine, the charismatic Islamic leader of the Justice and Charity movement, "Al Adl Wal Ihssan" in Arabic, had previously written a letter to King Hassan II in 1974: "Islam or the deluge." Yassine was placed in a mental institution, but later released. For the past ten years, he's been living in Salé, under house arrest. The possibility of his release has often been discussed, but it hasn't happened yet. His daughter, Nadia, acts as his spokesperson. Yes, his daughter, a woman . . .

Yassine's new letter made no mention of women, but it was obviously being sent out at that moment because of the great debate about the National Plan for Action, which was prompting Islamic groups to intervene. Members of the Justice and Charity movement wanted to make their presence felt, but they were doing so very astutely by broaching another topic.

The eighteen-page letter written by Sheik Abdessalam Yassine that appeared on the Internet site created by his movement was called "Memorandum to Whom It May Concern." The letter's distribution was timed to have an impact on the entire political community. It was, I believe, a declaration of war . . .

The "Memorandum" brings us back to the topic of Morocco's great debate: How do we deal with the past? We may not know how, but Sheik Abdessalam Yassine does, because he knows everything. He appealed directly to the king, whom he found likable and well-intentioned. He claimed he wanted to believe the king was sincere. He was aware that the king too had suffered from the previous reign, and said so: "Mohammed VI knows better than anyone about the brutal ways and 'castrated' language of the now dead king in his relations with Moroccans, be they his relatives and associates or his servants, because he himself had been subjected to them."

The rest of the letter was an unmitigated indictment of the past, of the previous regime, of Mohammed VI's father, the deceased Hassan II. It was a blatant accusation. Of what? Of "having led the country to the edge of the precipice . . . , this ship without a captain run adrift, this backward nation that Morocco has become." He quoted all the figures and statistics:

Morocco ranks 125th on the HDI (Human Development Index) according to the UNPD (United Nations Program for Development), well behind Algeria and Tunisia. Twelve million Moroccans live below the poverty level, earning less than ten *dirhams* (less than one dollar) per day per person. Three-fourths of salaried workers earn below minimum wage (1,600 *dirhams* per month). Salary ratios vary between 1 and 1,000 (while in Europe they vary between 1 and 10). Twenty-three percent of working-age Moroccans are unemployed. There are 100,000 unemployed degree holders. Fifty-three percent of Moroccans are illiterate.

How did things get so bad? Through a systematic pillaging of the country's wealth by the monarch and his clientele. Through the ONA (Omnium nord-africain), "the far-reaching network that Hassan II controlled," "a many-headed hydra, a bloodsucker that siphoned and continues to siphon off scandalous profits to pump them into the dead monarch's staggering fortune." "Everything in Morocco more or less belonged to that untouchable monster known as the ONA, and therefore to the king . . ." It happened through widespread corruption, bureaucratic red tape, drug trafficking, and fierce repression in the form of assassinations, kidnappings, and torture.

Who was behind it all? The trio that Sheik Abdessalam Yassine continued to denounce: Oufkir, Dlimi, and Basri. And first and foremost, King Hassan II.

What could be done now? The sheik was demanding that the young king (as well as his brothers and sisters) give back to the country what had been stolen from it, that he use the immense fortune that was his inheritance to pay off the debt crushing the country (36 percent of the GNP).

According to economists, the figures given for Morocco are accurate, those concerning the royal fortune cannot be verified, and the remedy that Yassine proposed is laughable.

The "Memorandum" ends with the following paragraph: "I wish the young king much strength and courage as I repeat in closing: in this turmoil, redeem your poor father by restoring to the people the wealth that is rightfully theirs. Redeem yourself! Repent! Fear the king of kings!"

I would have so loved to have seen Mohammed VI donate his fortune—or part of it—to those most in need: to the Tazmamart survivors, for example, to make amends for their horrible past; to the common people in the form of small loans in regions where the monarchy owns extensive property; to hospitals; to who knows what else. It wouldn't have done much to change the economic reality, but it would have been a symbolic gesture and would have yanked the rug out from under the populists . . . Maybe it's too late now; I don't know. If the king did it, Sheik Abdessalam Yassine and his "Memorandum to Whom It May Concern" would get the credit.

Nonetheless, I have to wonder if publishing the letter when the sheik did wasn't, in fact, an avowal of weakness: the fear of being outdone by other Islamic movements, and in particular, the Party for Justice and Development, which has seats in Parliament. Most of all, the fear that the tremendous popularity enjoyed by Mohammed VI, "the poor man's king," will deprive the Islamists of their breeding grounds for recruitment: the country's poor youths, be they from universities or shantytowns. That would explain why the attacks aimed at the king, who is so well-liked, were restrained and often treacherous in an understated way, while those aimed at his father, who was far from being liked, were extremely violent.

I wanted clarification. I decided to see Sheik Abdessalam Yassine's daughter, Nadia, who, as I said, is a kind of unofficial spokesperson for the movement. She agreed to meet me in front of the prison in Salé. "You and I are both quite familiar with prisons, aren't we?" she said, adding that she lived close by. The neighborhood was clean, quiet, and relatively new, yet traditional. The doors were framed with colorful mosaics. Her apartment was simple, sunny, and decorated mostly in blues. A painting on the wall, with the word for God in subdued gold letters on a blue background, caught my attention. I thought it was beautiful. Nadia had painted it herself.

She was very cordial. Her husband made an appearance, greeted me, then disappeared. Nadia is a pretty woman, quick to smile. That day, she was dressed in simple attire. She spoke perfect French, which she had learned as a young girl in French schools here. She explained that her father had encouraged his daughters to go to school, like the boys.

I had two important questions to ask her. I began:

"I believe Islam is tolerant and respectful of the 'people of the book.' So what is it that your movement, your father, and perhaps even you have against Jews?"

She answered: "Oh, we have nothing against Jews; but here in Morocco, they support the despotism of the Makhzen . . ."

"Some do, perhaps; that's true. We can talk about that in a minute. But what about the people in the *mellah*s,[5] in the cities, in the southern countryside, and all the Jews opposed to the

5. Translators' note: Jewish ghettos.

despotism of the Makhzen? There were others besides Abraham during the first decade of Morocco's independence."

"The people of the *mellah*s, the impoverished Jews, are a part of us, the Moroccan people. What you're saying is correct . . ."

"As for those who supported the despotism of the Makhzen — to use your phrase — why not fight them as political adversaries, instead of as Jews?"

Nadia thought for a moment, trying to remember the words used in the "Memorandum."

"That's true," she said. "We have to make the distinction and be more careful about the terms we use. It could offend the Jews and have repercussions for us."

"Yes, it could offend the Jews; that's for sure. And it could have repercussions for you because it justifies treating you as anti-Semitic. That's true, too. Will you speak to your father about it for me?"

"Yes, I will. Certain things need to be corrected . . ."

Nadia is an intelligent woman; I realized it right away. And I found her friendly. I asked my second question:

"I admire Islam's absence of clergy. I see that as a sign that every human being has a direct relationship with God. So it's a private matter, between God and each individual. What business does the government have getting involved in it?"

Nadia smiled and said: "If Islam, as we would like it to exist, were practiced as it should be, if all members of society were devout and respected what the Koran teaches — respected what we want to achieve through persuasion and education — there would be no need for external coercion, and the government would slowly fade out."

I thought back on the bygone days of the communist dream: the blissful transformation of society, the communist period which was in fact supposed to lead to the decline and eventual phasing out of the state. But persuasion turned into Gulags. And what has become of the hope of that era?

We continued our conversation, jumping from topic to topic.

"Yes, we're against the Plan for Action to Integrate Women in Development," Nadia said. "Why? Because it talks about international rights, about World Bank support, but never mentions our Islamic values, the identifying values of our culture. Can a bank, even and especially a world bank, build the happiness of all humanity? Granted, the Mudawwana needs to be changed: we don't support polygamy. It can remain in theory, but shouldn't be practiced. Repudiation shouldn't stay the way it is. Goods and possessions should be shared equally between men and women. As for the veil . . . In the privacy of the home, women can expose their femininity for their husbands, be beautiful, seductive, and tempting. In public, they should only be what they are for the public: engineers, teachers, saleswomen—in a word, citizens. They should be appreciated for that, not for their physical qualities. The veil is like the smocks and uniforms worn in schools and other such places. It eliminates social and sexual differences."

What could I say to that, since I was actually fond of the smocks we wore in grade school?

"We're for education, the education of the people of this country. We're against violence. We never want the situation to become like it is in Algeria."

I told her I sincerely hoped her father would soon be freed. She thanked me, and we kissed each other on both cheeks, as women always do. There's just one thing that bothers me. I believe she was sincere in what she said; but were the ideas she expressed the same as those of the other members of the movement? I don't know. But I do know that the need for government intervention to which Nadia alluded—so long as Muslims aren't true believers as defined by the Koran (the word of God handed down by the Prophet)—inevitably implies a desire to seize power to create a repressive, totalitarian society similar to the Stalinist state. And I know I can't agree with that.

Regardless, that night I told Abraham with a sigh: "You had a close call. One more hour with her, and I would have ended up joining the Justice and Charity movement . . ."

In late February, the league and councils of the ulamas of Morocco condemned Sheik Abdessalam Yassine's memorandum in the name of Islam, and more specifically in the name "of the Koran, the Sunna [i.e., tradition], and the unanimity of the *ummah*—in other words, the entire Islamic community."

৩

That brings us back to women, poor creatures that they are. All you men can breathe easily; the Mudawwana won't be changed. Naturally, the minister of Habous and Islamic Affairs asked the ulamas to calm down the situation in the mosques. He's a sovereign minister. That means the order, or recommendation, came from the top. Within the parties forming the government or supporting it, everyone agreed to postpone making changes to the personal status code, recognizing that any thoughts on the issue should stem from Islam, the state religion of Morocco. So they'll have to meet again, discuss it with other groups, and above all, take more time to think about it.

The personal status code, the Mudawwana, dates from the first year of independence—1958. They've already had fifty years to think about it . . .

So, all my sisters, will anything ever change? Of course it will, tomorrow . . .

A huge demonstration for women and their supporters was planned for March 12th in Rabat. I wondered if they'd be granted a demonstration permit.

❧ Past-Present:
The Survivors' Dinner

One day in Geneva, quite a while back—five or six years ago, I believe—I found out about the United Nations Voluntary Fund for Victims of Torture. I decided to solicit the organization's help, and the people there were very responsive. I told them about the Tazmamart survivors. They said I needed to fill out an application form, which I promptly did. Once the request had been reviewed by the fund's board of directors, money could be allocated to the torture victims. The granting of funding in such cases can either be kept secret or made public, depending on the political regimes of the countries where the victims reside. For years, it has been kept secret, but I want to make it public now by writing about it.

My friend Marie-Hélène and I, together with a lawyer, Mr. Bourdon, filed the papers to form the "Justice for Tazmamart" association, whose basic mission was to raise money for the survivors—money from the United Nations, but also wherever else we could find it. The Committee Against

Repression in Morocco, located in Brussels, contributed a sizable amount, and friends made donations. As soon as the Tazmamart survivors receive the indemnity provided for by the Moroccan government—which is under review by the Compensation Commission established in August of 1999—we will notify Geneva, and the association will be dissolved.

Marie-Hélène had a piano, and every year she and her husband, François, used to organize a private concert performed by volunteer musicians. They set up folding chairs and charged an admission fee that went to the Tazmamart survivors. It's very moving for me to recall those little concerts. Marie-Hélène selected the musical program. By way of introduction, I would tell the story of Tazmamart for the benefit of those who had never been to one of the concerts before; then I'd give updates on everyone's current situation. I can still see the faces of the regulars: Jeannine, who has since passed away; Heide; and François and Marie-Hélène's children—Rachel, Céline, and Lucas—who helped organize the event. After the concert, there was a buffet for everyone, musicians and audience alike.

Once the money was divided up and distributed to the Tazmamart survivors living in Morocco, the amount seemed rather paltry; but I believe the important thing for them was that it was a sign that the world hadn't forgotten about them, that they were registered somewhere, at the United Nations, and that it protected them in some way.

Marie-Hélène and François came to spend a few days with Abraham and me in Mohammedia. We decided to plan a dinner for the survivors, since Marie-Hélène and François had never met them in person. Reporters from France 3 TV came by in the afternoon to cover the story. Caroline Sinz was the program manager. Ten years earlier, in Paris and Geneva, Caroline and her crew used to report on the horrors of Tazmamart. That day, she too finally got to meet the survivors.

Moments of the past, different pasts, started merging with the present in my mind: a present that was becoming very complex.

Those who lived close by began to arrive for the dinner. It was the first visit for some. Among the guests was a man who had come to my apartment in Paris twenty years earlier with letters from his brother, who had disappeared. I was once more seeing him with my own eyes. My hands could touch him. Naturally, his father had come with him; and for a long time, I could see and hear only them and nothing else, because they marked the very beginning of this story—a beginning so engraved in my mind that I knew parts of the letters by heart. And now, here in this house so far away, the story was reaching its epilogue. Even before seeing those letters, I had begun searching for the prisoners who had vanished from the long-term prison in Kenitra. But at that time, I had no idea what they had been enduring for seven years.

During the dinner, the survivors told the story of how, after five years in prison, they were made to go outside to be reshuffled into different cells. The guards had never really seen them, because the cellblocks were always kept in total darkness. The men began staggering and falling in the bright light and open air. Never imagining the prisoners would be in such bad condition, the guards had armed themselves with clubs to prevent attacks, mutinies, or escapes. There was a deafening silence; then suddenly an officer yelled: "Put down your clubs and help them. Can't you see they can't even stand up?" They weren't able to walk anymore, and had to be carried by the guards. The worst-off of the men was put in a wheelbarrow, like a sack of potatoes.

Only four prisoners from Building Two—the worst cellblock—had survived, and one of them was with us that evening. Like the others, he had shrunk considerably in height, and his joints were knotted. I noticed he had trouble turning his head. But he was the most lighthearted of them all. He laughed as he told the most horrific stories, and sad as they were, he made us laugh too. There was much laughter during that dinner at Abraham's house—Abraham, who had spent fifteen months in Derb Moulay Cherif, seventeen years in prison, eight years in exile. We laughed with our guests, the survivors of Tazmamart, who had spent eighteen years in a secret prison, in cells that never saw the light of day, that no one visited, that no one left, and that reeked of excrement and death. When a prisoner was dying, the guards—always the same ones—refused to go into his cell because of the stench. They would ask another prisoner to go in their place; and that's how each man lived the death of his fellow prisoners.

Two guards—only two—took pity on them. They risked their lives, smuggling out notes to families and smuggling in whatever medicine they could. They saved the prisoners' lives. "If we get any compensation, we need to give them a cut," said one of the survivors in a loud voice. And another added, "And to the human rights organizations, too."

In 1984, one of the prisoners, Air Force Lieutenant Touil, started getting special treatment. His wife was American—there was an American base in Kenitra. When she got back to the United States, she did everything possible to pull administrative and legal strings. The U.S. ambassador in Rabat was allowed to meet with Touil privately. He came out of the meeting sheet-white, his teeth clenched. Since Touil was serving a twenty-year sentence, with no possibility of parole, the ambassador requested a special diet for him. After Touil returned to Tazmamart, he was given better food and allowed to bathe and sun himself daily in the courtyard, where a dog named Hinda kept him company.

Hinda had belonged to a Frenchman who liked to hunt. When he left Morocco, he gave the dog to a neighbor, who was also fond of hunting. The Frenchman had no idea that his neighbor was in charge of the Tazmamart camp. He didn't even know it existed. Eventually, the dog lost its sense of smell and was useless for hunting. Hinda's new master decided to punish her by putting her in jail, too—or rather, by confining her to the prison courtyard. The prisoners could hear the animal bark continually and paw at the door, trying to get help and escape.

When Touil went out into the courtyard for the first time, it was bliss for both of them. The dog no longer felt abandoned. Touil took care of it, washed it, and gave it affection. One time, for Aïd el-Kebir, a guard did the prisoners a favor: he left the doors open for fifteen minutes, both the cell doors and the doors of the building, so they could have a taste of fresh air and sunlight. It was his gift to them for the holiday. Hinda ran into the building, then into a cell, and started licking one of the prisoners. The dog ran into another cell, and still another, visiting all twenty-nine of them. If a prisoner lay dying at the back of his cell, the dog would go all the way in to find him. Otherwise, she would stop at the partially opened door to lick the prisoners standing there.

That's the story of Hinda—the story of a dog's compassion—told to us that evening by the ex-prisoners.

The special treatment Touil received made life all the more miserable for the other men who weren't as lucky. The door opening onto the fresh air and sunlight every day, the smell of the food he was served were constant reminders of what they were being deprived of, and it was very hard on them. It was equally hard on Touil because he was a good man, and the prisoners were his friends. Each morning, he gave a spoonful of jam to Hamida, the youngest and most obliging of the inmates. Another ration was distributed to the other prisoners, each in turn. When Ahmed's turn came, he put his three spoonfuls of jam on the edge of his plate. The cell was in total darkness. Later, when he went to eat the jam, he groped around for the plate on one side of the cell, then on the other, but couldn't find it. Frustrated, he gave up, went over to the stone ledge, and sat down—right on the plate . . .

Everyone was doubled over with laughter.

What was behind their laughter and their stories? What was deep inside them? One of the guests—the captain—was talking. Occasionally he'd laugh. His eyes were wells of suffering—black, unfathomable. While he was incarcerated in Tazmamart, he wrote a sorrowful and extremely beautiful poem. Sadly, I think he'd write the same poem today. People never forget. All they can do is learn to live with their memories.

ॐ

In the course of the last ten years, the survivors have married. Some have had children; some have pursued an education. Very few have found work. They feel good when they're together because of what they've been through: the long years they endured in darkness, hunger, and cold—breathing the stench of death.

Are we going to forget the past? Those well-dressed, closely-shaven, courteous men conversing with us that evening were our guests. One of them brought me flowers, another a dish of pastries. Yet for eighteen years, they'd been unkempt, dressed in rags, bent over, their hair and beards uncut, their nails like claws. They had even invented a language so they could talk among themselves without being understood by the guards, who thought they'd gone mad.

Before being released on September 15, 1991, the prisoners in Building One watched the four survivors of Building Two being moved to their cellblock. They were unrecognizable. It was a chillingly frightful sight. The prisoners couldn't tell if the four frail shadows stumbling before their eyes—and who were once their brothers—were still human . . .

I later found out that the day after the dinner, a survivor— one of the most traumatized by the prison experience—had been questioned by an agent from the Ministry of the Interior about his links with television reporters and foreign media. Things hadn't changed. Different men were working at the Ministry of the Interior, but the same old attitudes prevailed. But why? After all, my book on Tazmamart had been published here in Arabic. One of the survivors recounted his experiences in the newspaper published by the USFP, the prime minister's social democratic party. Everything has been disclosed; everything has been revealed. And the survivors' files are being reviewed by the Compensation Commission. So why?

⌀

In glancing over the day's headlines, I noticed the front-page story in the weekly paper, *Le Journal:* "Adib to Be Tried by Order of the King." Adib was the aviation captain who exposed corruption in the military and, to add to the scandal, did so in a foreign newspaper—France's *Le Monde.* He gave the newspaper permission to print his name. *Le Journal* chronicled the "affair": On December 10, 1999, the king ordered that Captain Adib be "brought before the royal armed forces' permanent military court for disobeying orders and slandering the army." Adib's article appeared in *Le Monde* on December 16, so the sanction wasn't linked to its publication, but rather something else. But what? Word had it that the officer denounced by Adib for stealing and selling fuel had been punished; but word also had it that he'd been released before completing half his sentence. It's likewise known that, at the time, Captain Adib had asked to speak to the king—the army's commander-in-chief and therefore Adib's highest superior officer. He wasn't seen by the king, but by his cabinet head, Fouad Ali El Himma, instead. Did Adib simply want to talk to the king about a routine case of fuel theft? Many people think not; they think that it was about something more— something that was never brought out in the open—and that the trial, which was the result of military pressure, was supposed to serve as an example.

For some, the captain's action was a form of bribery that had to be squelched; for others, it was, on the contrary, a normal and respectable move: a desire to inform the army's commander-in-chief, the king. The head of the royal cabinet couldn't take the king's place, because he isn't a member of the military. The military court refused to let him testify as a witness, just as it refused to disqualify one of the members of the court for potential bias since he was one of the officers Captain Adib had denounced for trafficking; just as it denied all requests made by the defense—namely, that it not be a closed hearing, that witnesses be allowed to testify, and that Captain Adib be released provisionally.

ç

The press had the freedom and courage to broach issues as sensitive as this—doubly sensitive since it involved both the army and the monarchy. Yet at the same time, two Moroccan papers, as well as an issue of *Jeune Afrique* magazine, were stopped at customs. They contained articles which I later read and didn't find particularly dangerous to the stability of the kingdom. Islamic papers were seized; an Islamic activist was arrested—then released—for having distributed Sheik Abdessalam Yassine's "Memorandum to Whom It May Concern." The sheik's family was temporarily denied the passports they needed to make the pilgrimage to Mecca. Even an issue of the French paper *Le Figaro* was pulled from distribution.

I learned that the most zealous Moroccan TV announcer was relieved of his duties and replaced. His zeal was such that when he announced Hassan II's death in July, he turned his face and hid his tears with his hand, and made the very same gesture during each subsequent newscast. But when will they replace the *wali,* the authority-wielding official who controls all television operations?

One of my friends, Ahmed Marzouki, a Tazmamart survivor, even told me he had been questioned by a *moqqadem*— one of fifty thousand "police" agents who have extensive legal powers to infiltrate and patrol every neighborhood in cities across Morocco, as well as all the villages in the countryside, and who then report what they find out to their superiors. This particular agent wanted to know why I'd been to Ahmed's house the day before: "Why was that woman at your house? Why did she come? What's she trying to do?"

It was true that I'd had lunch the day before with Ahmed and his wife in their home. I wanted to see their new nine-month-old son. Ahmed is such an exemplary man—so honest, courageous, and devout. After eighteen years in Tazmamart, his marriage and the birth of his child were, to my mind, strong symbols of hope, of confidence in humanity—and also in the future of this country.

Ahmed handled the situation with the *moqqadem* very well. He asked to see the document that denied him the right to talk to me. After all, I had entered Morocco legally and without any restrictions. He also drafted a communiqué that was sent to human rights organizations and published in the papers. I took action too, by informing friends of mine in the government about what had happened. I let them know that the thought that my presence could put someone in danger was unbearable to me—especially someone more vulnerable than I was, and who'd already suffered so much.

The next day, we found out that the *moqqadem* had been dismissed.

༄

I'm well aware that it's impossible to go from one regime to another overnight, change the notion of authority in people's minds so quickly, monitor every level of decision making within the ministries and service sectors, keep overzealousness in check, and prevent individuals from taking things into their own hands. But there are sad days. This was one of them.

Overzealousness at local levels, old habits that won't die, ignorance and total incomprehension of the fact that a page has finally been turned—there's a bit of all that behind the little blunders committed daily in Morocco. But any reminder of the past casts a shadow over our hope. That's a fact.

The days are a conglomeration of all those things. There are setbacks, there is stagnation, and there is progress too. One sad day? A string of sad days? I don't know anymore . . .

Captain Adib was sentenced to five years in prison: the maximum sentence. He was barred from the Moroccan military. He was young, thirty-two, and boyishly good-looking. His lawyers maintained that the trial had been conducted in an unacceptable manner.

Yes, the day he was sentenced was a sad day.

A friend, an American diplomat, called me from France. I asked him if they were still optimistic about the changes brewing in Morocco. He said yes, that they were optimistic at the Department of State. But he added: "Too bad there was that business about the military man. Really too bad. A five-year sentence is too much . . ." That's what my American friend told me. You can check for yourself. The people tapping my phone line will confirm it for you. For once, I have to agree with the U.S. Department of State.

We are under the rule of Creon. I know that, and I understand. Creon wanted to initiate reforms in his native city of Thebes for the welfare of the people, for everyone's welfare. His intentions were good. Antigone, his niece, had two brothers, Eteocles and Polynices, who plotted against him and were killed. To set an example, Creon ordered that their bodies be left unburied, like dogs. That went against the prevailing ethics and religion. Every morning, before sunrise, Antigone walked out onto the plain alone and scraped the soil with her hands to cover her brothers' bodies. Every morning—until she was caught in the act by Creon's guards and brought before him. She had risked her life—and knew it, because Creon had proclaimed that anyone who tried to bury the dead brothers would be condemned to death.

I understand Creon: the Creon of antiquity—of Thebes—and all the Creons of today. I do. I'm not defending instigators; I'm really not—especially those who'd like to see the changes currently taking place fail. Yet something deep inside me believes that every society needs an Antigone.

❧

In his capacity as commander-in-chief, King Mohammed VI left Rabat to inspect the troops at several military sites in the Tafilalt. That's something his father hadn't done, perhaps because the endeavor was too strenuous for him, given his age and poor health. Ever since the 1971 and 1972 coups, the army had had free rein. It was in charge of security along the borders and keeping law and order within the country, but some military leaders managed their affairs as they saw fit, and in ways that were most advantageous for themselves.

෴

Still no rain. It was surely going to be a dry year, because not only did it need to rain, but the rain had to come at the right time. Farmers in eastern Morocco had already started sending their livestock to the Fez and Meknes regions. Not because eastern Morocco got less rain than the rest of the country — it hadn't rained anywhere — but because eastern Morocco had been suffering from a severe rainfall shortage over the last several years. The farmers would have to sell the animals before the Aïd holiday.

Aïd el-Adha, the feast of the sacrifice of Abraham: here in Morocco, it's called Aïd el-Kebir, the great feast, or the Feast of the Lamb. Tradition dictates that every family slaughter a lamb after the Commander of the Faithful, the king himself, slaughters his own lamb in public. Four and a half million lambs are killed on that day. It's a blessed day for farmers, and they all work hard for the event.

But the Muslims go by a lunar calendar, so the holidays move ahead about ten days a year in relation to the solar calendar. The seasons, which are clearly delineated by the solar calendar, aren't taken into account. But the rains and grazing fields are influenced by the seasons. Consequently, the Aïd can fall at a good time or a bad time.

Many people would like to see the Commander of the Faithful limit the feast to a symbolic sacrifice: one lamb per neighborhood, or poultry instead of lamb. It's permitted by the Islamic religion. But for poor families who stretch themselves to the limit to buy a lamb, it remains a holiday replete with several days of revelry and feasting. And it's an accepted, ritualistic tradition. A real holiday . . .

That year, banks were ordered to tighten up on credit. Local branches had to refer all cost overruns to the central office, which made the final decision and usually denied authorization. Salary advances that year, however, were granted to rank-and-file employees.

The Aïd was coming. The exact date would only be announced ten days beforehand, but we knew it would be around the 17th of March. Even if it rained over the next two weeks, the grass wouldn't have enough time to grow to fatten the animals. So what could be done?

The ulamas prayed for rain—because that's what the weather report was predicting, and they'd heard it. So was it going to happen? The ulamas don't pray in vain. The rabbis followed suit: solemn supplications were made in all the synagogues. Unfortunately, the ulamas and rabbis failed. The meteorologists seemed to have been mistaken, and the farmers had to set their flocks free to graze in fields where the wheat was still green.

ej

In this Morocco that I love so much, there are days, in any case, when I feel locked in by the country's shores and closed borders, cut off from everything. It's curled up around itself. Its back is turned to the rest of the world. Consequently, it can't see to what extent the world is stirring, waking, and stretching. Morocco is still dozing. It has yet to get up and get going. And it's not just because nature is so stingy with the rainfall, nor is it due to the reticence of foreign investors. There's an internal weightiness here, an inertia that saps energy and blocks results. Even the country's intellectuals, absorbed by their work in their own disciplines, off in their own corners, haven't succeeded in creating ties among themselves. There are no networks or bases to put individuals in touch with one another so they can share ideas and solutions in sync with the country's identity and culture—nothing to make action and reaction possible. That's how nations move forward: by observing each other, comparing, confronting, working, persevering—and suffering.

I really don't know why it is that on these days that seem so gray despite the bright blue sky, my thoughts don't turn to Europe or France. No; it's Africa that I miss. Intensely so—deeply so. I miss the Africa that Morocco doesn't know: the poorest, bloodiest, most destitute Africa. But it's also so beautiful, so rich in human potential. And I've never felt stifled there the way I do here.

✑ Return to Tangier

This story is drawing to a close. I can't continue to live and write, write and live as I've been doing for the past four months. The "living" phase included a trip to Tangier, and I'll bring this story to an end with my account of it: Tangier was my point of arrival in the early 1960s, after Morocco became independent. I had come with my two oldest children, Christophe and Lise, who were still quite young, to teach history and geography at the Ibn-el-Khatib school. I had tremendous hope for the country. And tremendous hope for my partner and me, for the love that was beginning. The dazzle of new discoveries seemed like a promise of happiness.

In those days, quite a few French people, myself included, set out for burgeoning countries that had been newly liberated from the weight of colonialism. They went to repair the damage of decades past—or so they thought. By the time I left Tangier four years later, to teach at the Mohammed v school in Casablanca, I'd been married at the French Consulate on the Place de France; I'd given birth to a third child,

Lucile; and my hopes had been replaced by a great feeling of anger.

For four years, day after day, I had discovered Tangier and come to love it passionately. Yes, passionately—the beauty of the surroundings, the natural beauty there: the hills, sea and ocean, sand and rocks, eucalyptus, datura, and rubber trees. Have you ever seen a tree more beautiful than the rubber tree in the Mendoubia Gardens on the Grand Socco square? I love the beauty of the city—its houses and streets of all kinds, dating from all eras. The beauty of the Morocco of the past: Spanish Morocco, Jewish Moroccan families, the international period, and the Old Mountain houses—each harboring, as does every bend in the road, the fond memory of a writer.

Yes, I was captivated by the beauty of the surroundings and by my students' interest in learning, their interest in knowledge—a knowledge that, until then, had been denied them, but which seemed within their reach as a result of the country's independence. An incredible hope, an incredible love: such is my recollection of those years in Tangier. And that love, born in Tangier, grew to encompass the entire country.

When I left Tangier in 1967, hope had died three times: On March 23, 1965, when the army opened fire on pupils demonstrating in the streets of Casablanca against a government reform that limited their access to knowledge, excluded the poorest of them, and condemned those who believed it was possible to rise above poverty to sink to its most abject level. On October 29, 1965, when Mehdi Ben Barka was kidnapped in the heart of Paris and vanished forever. In June, 1967, when in the span of six days, Israel triumphed over Jamal Abdel Nasser, the Egyptian army, Arab nationalism, and the Palestinians' hope of regaining their homeland and their rights. The rejoicing and laughter of French Zionists still echoes in my mind.

ᘓ

People had warned me: "It's been thirty years since you've seen Tangier. You'll be disappointed. Everything's changed. It's dirty, run-down; the sidewalks are all broken up. You won't recognize a thing . . ." But I recognized everything: the street where the school used to be (although the school's not there anymore); the street where I used to live; the Spanish hospital where Lucile was born; the Grand Socco square, with the market entrance off to the right. I would have liked to go inside the market, to find the stall of the fish vendor whose sign still read: "*carne de ballena.*" I recognized the white boats coming and going between the two continents, the Place de France and the cafés around it, and the lingering yellow clusters of mimosa. Someday I'll come back to see the blue irises blooming on the hills.

There stands a tree in Mendoubia Gardens whose branches and roots mingle in a silent and motionless entanglement. Nearby is a plaque commemorating the visit made by Mohammed v and his daughter, Lalla Aïcha, on April 9, 1947. Although there's no plaque for German Emperor Wilhelm II, there are a number of pictures of him riding horseback up the street leading from the port and onto the Grand Socco square at the Mendoubia Gardens entrance. He had come to give a speech and to chart out Germany's plans for Morocco, which conflicted with those of France.

All of you who told me "You'll be disappointed . . ." said that because you've lost your youth. You can no longer find it in Tangier. I didn't find mine there either. But I did find my former students, and they too have lost their youth. Yet even without it, or perhaps by virtue of it, we found each other again, after all the years that had gone by—those dark years of repression in Morocco.

ৎ

The rally Abraham and I attended in Tangier was at the Mauritania movie theater near the Fez market. I used to take my children to the Mauritania back when we were naive, easy-to-please moviegoers. *Lawrence of Arabia* had entranced us. On the day of the rally, the theater was filled to capacity. There were people seated and standing on both levels—over a thousand if I'm not mistaken (I'm in the habit of doing head-counts). Many of my former students came up to me to introduce themselves and say hello.

A man slipped me a piece of paper and left. I unfolded it and read: "How about setting up an alumni association for students who attended the school back then?" I smiled and felt like saying: "Yes," an association called "Hope," the hope of those days gone by. Is it still possible? Is it already possible? "Still." "Already." Thirty years have elapsed between those two words: thirty years of poverty, torture, imprisonment; thirty dark years. An abyss . . . Will we be able to fill that void? Will we at least be able to forget it existed? The note was addressed to "Our Christine." All of you know that, as far as I'm concerned, Tangier will always be "our Tangier."

Soon after I returned to France in 1976, I was invited to Brussels to take part in a huge rally protesting the repression in Morocco. It had been organized by resistance committees there that, for years, had been holding up the truth for all the world to see. I remember how much we accomplished with no funding (except for the money we put in ourselves), and without a paid staff or permanent employees. It was the thankless work of activists, carried out evenings and on weekends, after we'd finished the work we all had to do to earn a living. I didn't know at the time that Belgium was the northern destination for emigrants from Tangier. That was why I saw so many of my former Moroccan students in the room in Brussels, smiling and waving at me . . .

And again in February 2000, at the rally here in Tangier, I saw many of my former students smiling at me. The first row was the place of honor reserved for ex-political prisoners. It was for those same people that the 1976 meeting in Brussels had been organized while their trial was taking place. That trial would ultimately condemn their young lives collectively to three thousand years in prison. As they were called to the podium at the Tangier rally, the audience applauded and gave them a standing ovation. Even though those men had spent their youth in the kingdom's prisons, they were the ones who came out victorious.

ভ

A few days ago, in the newspapers, a former police chief asked for forgiveness from all the people he had tortured. It was the top story in *Le Journal.* And one of the former officials responsible for the horrors in Tazmamart has also supposedly shown remorse and rediscovered the religious devotion he'd lost. "You can't be a good Muslim and do what I do," he used to mutter.

ʕ

During his childhood and adolescence, Abraham spent his vacations in Tangier with an aunt who had money but no children. He'd go to the beach, and his aunt would meet him there to buy some fish for lunch from a local fisherman. Then they would drive back to her house in Mçalla. Abraham can still remember the large winding staircase and the pretty garden behind the house. They'd have tea in the afternoon at a café on the Old Mountain, overlooking the straits. The name of the café was "Farah," which means "happiness." I hope he was able to see those places again, but I seriously doubt it. His memory is so good, though, that he really doesn't need to. And besides, his life is elsewhere. Yet I know all that is a part of him.

ʕ

The Tangier rally continued. Different people spoke in turn, as the audience applauded loudly. They gave Abraham a book, and Rabea offered me a lovely bouquet of flowers. Rabea, my dearest Rabea. I don't know why it is, but I always call you "my dearest" when I think of you. Do you remember, as I do, the visiting room at the prison in Kenitra, and the guard who wanted to search us one evening in the light of the setting sun because he was angry to see us there, angry that we were so determined and unwavering? When it was Abraham's turn to address the audience, there was a hushed silence. Everyone was captivated. He declared his support for all united left-wing candidates in the 2002 legislative elections. There was thunderous applause. Later, I asked him: "Abraham, are you going to support them? For sure?" "Yes, I am. For sure . . ."

After the rally was over, a friend said to me: "It was odd, and really very beautiful, to see the two of you at the center of the platform for such a typically Moroccan meeting, and to see all those people together around you at last, around a Jew and a *nasrania*." That's a difficult word to translate. It means "Christian"—or rather "foreigner," because it's not possible to be both Christian and Moroccan. The idea that someone might not have a religion is unheard of, at least at the present time. Was it really typical of Morocco? Or was it just a one-day miracle that happened in Tangier?

ᖋ

We took the Old Mountain road with a friend of mine. It sounds so much nicer in Spanish: *el monte viejo.* We stopped near a very long wall that had been painted blue. There were breaks in the wall where you could see the ocean, and it was even bluer. To the right, going up the road, there were paths as straight as ladders leading down to the sea between the houses and walled gardens. They were so straight and vertical that only the upper portions were visible, barely a few yards in length. At the bottom, all the way down, stretched the ocean, but it was too far away for us to hear the pounding of the waves. A man appeared nearby. He was coming up a path and seemed to have emerged from the water. As I looked around, I recognized every one of the huge old eucalyptus trees growing along the slope. They were the same trees I'd seen there thirty years earlier. Rooted as they were on the furthest tip of the continent, they too seemed to be emerging from the silent waters of the straits. The water is a mixture of colors: the Atlantic has its own particular shades, as does the Mediterranean. I remember how, for fun, I used to try to find the color of my children's eyes in the varying tones of the blue water: the pale blue of Christophe's eyes, the blue-green of Lise's, and the deeper blue of Lucile's.

The straits hadn't changed, but I had. And I was seeing them differently. Although their colors were as beautiful as ever in their eternal turbulence, I could no longer find amusement in them. That's because I know now that those waters have swallowed up too many hopes in the black of night. So many young Moroccans, Algerians, and Africans, isolated from one another in their daily lives to the point that they aren't even aware of each other's existence, come together for the first time along these southern shores, waiting for smugglers to take them in their *"pateras"* —rowboats and motorboats that leave each night to cross the straits. Many sink on the way. Before leaving, the passengers of those doomed boats share what little food they have and talk awhile about the northern shore, glimpsed in the evening light. They speak of the naive plans they have, and try to negotiate a better price for their passage to Europe. Then, knocked overboard by the currents caused by the clash of the sea's low waves with the ocean's high swells, they all perish—together.

No, it's not the straits that have changed; their beauty is the same. I'm the one who has changed over the course of these dark decades. And I'll continue to change—along with this country, as it shows signs of life, comes out of its sluggishness, and wakes at last, responding to its own needs. That's my most fervent hope. Words have been swirling in my head for days—swirling around feelings of hope and concern.

Two demonstrations were authorized to take place on Sunday, March 12, 2000: one in Rabat for women's rights, the other an Islamic march in Casablanca to defend family values. Both got underway on the same day, at the same time—10 A.M.—sixty miles from each other. One march raised concern; the other, hope. There was a big crowd in Casablanca (the night before, the Islamists held a huge rally at the Mohammed v Stadium, practically in the heart of the city). Stocked with sandwiches and lemonade, hordes of demonstrators arrived by the busload from all over Morocco. Many of them were young. The men and women marched separately, using megaphones and chanting non-violent slogans. The entire demonstration was very well organized.

In Rabat, the demonstration was also sizable, but the men and women marched together, and it was very spontaneous, very enthusiastic, and above all very lively. It had been years since there had been such a display of feverish excitement. No one thought it would ever be possible again. All sorts of people joined in support of the women and left-wing activists: teachers, business owners, fathers carrying children on their shoulders, intellectuals . . . The dense, unrestrained crowd filled the sprawling Mohammed v Avenue from Bab el-Hadd to the train station, and from there all the way to Pietri

Square. Morocco had changed since the summer of 1999, and women celebrated the change openly in the streets of Rabat in the spring of 2000.

Friends from Casablanca who had gone to Rabat stopped by the house on the way back, to tell us about "their" march and to conjecture about the number of demonstrators . . . And that too was lively, enthusiastic, and exuberant. We hugged each other on the doorstep, in front of the ocean waves. That night, hope had won out—a hope almost free of concern. Almost—under the hopelessly blue sky . . .

I believe this story is finished. It was merely intended to be an account. Perhaps it's even less than that: just a letter from Morocco to my friends in France and elsewhere. Less than an account, but at the same time more than one, because it was written for the people I love, who have followed every development of this long story right up to Abraham Serfaty's return, at last, to his homeland—Morocco.